IMPACT!

IMPACT!

Social Entrepreneurship and the Lasting Legacy

Natasha M Palumbo

Eternal Enterprise Publishing

Copyright © 2020 by Natasha M Palumbo

All rights reserved. This book or any portion thereof may not be reproduced or used in any manner whatsoever without the express written permission of the publisher except for the use of brief quotations in a book review or scholarly journal.

First Printing: 2019

Second Edition Printing: 2020

ISBN: 978-1-7344905-2-7

Author Bio Photograph By: Juan Padilla with Luxus Photos

Book Cover Designed By: Joanne Jenkins and Natasha Palumbo with Ldy Bug Images

Eternal Enterprise Publishing
Sacramento, CA Ordering Information:

Special discounts are available on quantity purchases by corporations, associations, educators, and others. For details, contact the publisher at the above listed address.

U.S. trade bookstores and wholesalers:
Please contact Natasha M Palumbo
Tel: (916) 470-3330 or email natasha@entrepreneurshipempowered.com

Dedication

To my beautiful children, Allan and Annabella, I will love you for all time and eternity. Remember to always love and share your gifts with the world. We are the STEEL Legacy. We have been chosen to make an IMPACT and to carry the light in a dark world. Live an EMPOWERED LIFE and encourage others to do the same.

Contents

Acknowledgments viii
Preface ix
Introduction: IMPACT! 1
Chapter 1: Social Entrepreneurship: The Movement 11
Chapter 2: The Mind of a Social Entrepreneur 19
Chapter 3: Ethics: The Core of Social Entrepreneurship ... 31
Chapter 4: Legal Structures, Business Planning, and Intellectual Property 43
Chapter 5: Marketing and Branding 75
Chapter 6: Funding Your Social Venture 103
Chapter 7: Leadership, Human Capital, and Volunteers . 123
Chapter 8: Leaving a Legacy 141
Why Statement and Vision Board 151
Steps to Form an LLC 153
Business Legal Structures 155
Business Plan Template 157
Marketing Plan 160
Income Statement, Balance Sheet, and Cash Flow 162
Accounting Terms 163
Employee Identification Number 165
Answer Key 166
References and Resources 167
About the Author 170

Acknowledgments

Father God, I thank You for the beautiful gift of life, Your eternal love, and amazing grace. Without You, I am nothing. Through You, I am Natasha M Palumbo, the daughter of the Most High. All honor and glory to Your name. Thank you for the gift to write and share my story with the world. It is an honor to be used by You.

To all the people who have helped me over the years with homeless outreaches and all the work it takes to make them happen, I could not have served without each of you. A special thank you to Chic, Ann, Ruthie, Simone, Sandie, Denise, and Rodney. You have been faithful to the call to serve, not only in the STEEL Legacy, but in your daily lives. You all have a servant's heart, and I am eternally grateful that you share yourselves. I know that I can depend on you to come and labor with me as we serve together.

To my best friend, Joanne Jenkins, thank you for being the one true person outside of my children that I trust with all of me. Thank you for all the support, not only for the time you have given to me during the writing of my book, but for all the constant support in my life. I am grateful for you. You are not only my best friend, you are my sister.

To my earthly angel, who shall remain unnamed, I am eternally grateful, and I pray you receive a thousand back for all you have done for me. You believe in me and see the vision that God has revealed to me. Thank you is simply not enough but for now it will have to do.

To the generations that have yet to enter the world. It is for you and my children that I work to break the generational curses and plant the blessings. May you read this book one day and know that I wrote it with you in mind. I love you with an everlasting love. You, too, are part of the STEEL Legacy.

Preface

To the reader, I want to thank you for your support. You will find a wealth of information in this book. *IMPACT* is full of up-to-date tools, strategies, and resources that will help you in life and business.

I am in the business of building up people who build businesses. I am honored to be able to help you build, too. You may visit my website at the address listed below. There you will find all the services and products I offer. In addition to my business website, I am also providing my social entrepreneurship website. I will be telling you more about that organization in the book, so the details are there for you to read, but I do encourage you to take a look at both websites to learn more about me.

I am a business adjunct professor for several colleges in the state of California, as well as a coach and consultant. I have been an entrepreneur since 2002. I am passionate not only about business, but education. In addition to teaching, I host several workshops in the U.S. I would love for you to connect with me. You can find me on both LinkedIn and Instagram @ Natasha M Palumbo.

Be well,
Natasha M Palumbo, MBA

Author, Coach, Consultant, and Speaker
Entrepreneur – Educator – Empowered

www.entrepreneurshipempowered.com
www.steellegacy.org

x

Introduction
IMPACT!

"The heart of human excellence often begins to beat when you discover a pursuit that absorbs you, frees you, challenges you, or gives you a sense of meaning, joy, or passion."

—Terry Orlick, educator and author

Did you know there is a calling on your life? Do you realize you have a great purpose? Do you know you were destined to make an IMPACT? Well, I am here to tell you yes to all of the above. I am here to encourage you in your calling, purpose, and give you the tools needed to help you build a legacy that will outlast time. One that will not only make an IMPACT in your lifetime, but for generations still to come.

I have the knowledge and experience to withstand and overcome the most humbling of universal human experiences of poverty, discrimination, neglect, and abuse. I have faced more in the first two decades of my life than most humans ever will. Unfortunately, that is not where my abuse stopped. I continued to suffer from all kinds of side effects. I have battled depression, low self-esteem, worthlessness, anger, self-hatred, and the list goes on. I am an empath and can attract takers. I never knew that I had rights to my NO. Though I have come very far, I am still a work in progress.

Education has been the scaffolding for the metamorphosis of my life. I am a firm believer in higher education, which is why I am a college professor. Without question, it has been my saving grace. I am the first in my family to hold a master's degree, let alone be a woman in that category. I have been chosen in this life to be a generational curse breaker and generational blessing maker. The IMPACT I have is profound. My life saves lives. Because I suffered, I now get to see lives transform right before my eyes. I get to see curses break and blessings be born. I get to experience a life I could not have even imagined. I get to inspire, and, more importantly, EMPOWER!

I talk and write about the elephant in the room, and I do so with no shame or regret. I start with my story. There is power in a story. Look at Hollywood. Nothing but stories. We cannot wait for a new one to arrive. Whether it be a play, a movie, or a TV show, we love a good story. Well, our lives are just that: a story. We are the main character, the villain, and the hero. Yes, you read that right. We can be the villain in our own stories. This is something that I need you to understand, especially as you begin working more and more with people. Did you know that we have anywhere between 12,000 and 60,000 thoughts per day? Did you know that 80% of those thoughts are negative? This is why I say that we, too, are the villains in our own story.

My story is that I have endured decades upon decades of trauma. I am a trauma expert—not because of some fancy degree, but because I endured. Everyone in the world has trauma: primary, secondary, or both. Just like no one gets out alive, no one gets away trauma-free. I have done intense work to heal and be free of the torture of trauma and the torture of wounded emotion. Logic will never win over wounded emotion. You must become emotionally intelligent. Then, and only then, will your logic win. Emotional intelligence allows you the space you need to hold emotion for yourself and then move forward in the facts of the case. You can have a deeper understanding of others by having high emotional intelligence (EI). You will see that I will weave EI throughout this book time and time again because it is that important. Especially in social entrepreneurship. I will go in depth into what social entrepreneurship is in the next chapter. If you are reading this book, then you have some interest in social entrepreneurship and you have a burning desire in your heart to make the world a better place. That is the core of social entrepreneurship. We fight the wicked problems of the world. We believe we can and will make a difference—an IMPACT!

"True happiness is not attained through self-gratification, but through fidelity to a worthy purpose."

—Helen Keller, author and activist

I have been a social entrepreneur since 2003. That is when I began serving the homeless. My core business, Start To Finish Files (STFF), also has a social component to it as well. It is a legal and medical copy service specializing in Social Security disability law. I have owned STFF since 2002. I began working for STFF in 1999 while I was going to school to be a high school photography teacher. The man I worked for decided he was going to go back to school to earn his PhD in economics. Little did I know this would be one moment for me that changed a thousand after it. I was a welfare mom living on a limited income. I only made about a thousand a month working, and I used my financial aid money to help support myself and my son. I am 100% a single mommy and I received very little child support, but little is much if God is in it.

Dan, the man I worked for, knew I had very little. He also knew I was a loyal employee and a solid worker. He could see that I had drive and that I was pursuing my goals with rigor. I was educating myself, raising my son independently, and pulling myself up and out of the pit that was trying to bury me. I was an overcomer. When he told me he was going to sell STFF, I said, *"Please, if there is any way for me to buy it, may we please explore those options?"* I, however, was poor. I couldn't buy a business with food stamps and a government check. Nope, that wasn't going to work. No one was going to loan me the money, either. After trying different things, I was beginning to feel hopeless that I didn't have a chance.

Then, one Sunday morning, I was just getting out of the shower, and the phone rang. Dripping wet, wrapped in a towel, I answered it.

"Hello?"

"Natasha, it's Dan. After much thought, I have decided I am going to sell you the business. I know you don't have the means to pay for it, so I am going to set you up with a payment plan. I am going to sell it to you for $20,000, and I will give you $4,000 start-up cash—$2,000 one month, $2,000 the next. There is enough money being generated by the business that you'll be able to pay the business off in two years, pay all expenses, and still make a nice profit. It is yours."

I could not even speak. Tears were pouring down my face. I was a welfare mom. I had stood in food lines to feed my son. Picked through moldy bread and rotten vegetables just to find something edible for us to eat. And now I was going to be the owner of a thriving business. Are you freaking kidding me right now?!

On July 16, 2002, I became the new owner of STFF, and it became my new legal name. I purchased the business with six locations in half the state of California, a small staff, some equipment, all the clients, and the name. Part of the agreement when Dan sold me the business was that he would continue to be a mentor to me. I was able to call on him whenever I needed to. He had advised me that this business had great growth potential. Well, I am a LION, and telling a LION that there is potential for growth means let's go get it! And that is just what I did. I wasted no time expanding STFF with my truest and most trustworthy employee, Joanne Jenkins, and a beautiful team of other wonderful people. I was able to grow STFF from six locations in half the state of California to twenty-seven locations in five states. I had an incredible run, but then the tide shifted. Paper records dissolved, and my business began to decline. There was nothing I could do but continue to reinvent myself. I learned how to scan records, and today I still scan records. I bid on contracts, and I won them. I then learned the law itself and had a short run as a non-attorney representative. Nothing was like the glory days of STFF.

During the downhill slump, I turned my attention to earning my master's degree. The main reason being I knew I could teach. If you recall me stating earlier, I was going to school to be a high school photography teacher. I actually have a K-12 education background, which serves me well today. I have always been a teacher. It is what I played when I was little, and it is one of my strongest gifts. I knew that if I earned my master's degree, I could teach at the college level. I had so much experience already, I thought, *This is a great fit for me. I will become a business professor.* In 2010, I graduated with my Master's in Business Administration (MBA) and hit the ground running.

I applied everywhere to no avail. The dice of life will toss you a no time and time again. Being told no can feel like a prison sentence.... Until you learn this one Palumbo Principle: *You have rights to your "NO," and your "YES" is undeniable.* When those dice come rolling your way with the words NO on them, I want you to pick them up, shake them in your hands, spit on them if you must, then throw them back to this world, and, with everything you have inside of you, say, "MY YES IS UNDENIABLE." Then keep it moving. Your yes is far more powerful than any no you will receive.

Today I am not only a college professor and Empowered Entrepreneur, but I am also an author, coach, consultant, and speaker. I am also a publisher. I now have three books under my belt, including this one. I have many more yet to come. I have reached thousands of students and have made a lasting IMPACT in their lives. What is for me will never be kept from me. This is true for you as well. Don't ever give up on the dream that has been placed inside you. It will take time to see the fruits of your labor, but if you faint not, you will see it. I can tell you from my own personal experience that it has all been worth it. All the abuse I endured. All the trials. All the tribulations. All the rejection. All the pain. All the good and the bad. It is my story. My life saves lives, and so does yours. Don't ever negate your beautiful heart. My heart is so amazing despite being treated with such cruel, inhuman acts. I hold deep compassion for all, including those who have done me wrong and abused me. I love deeply, and I love hard.

Along my journey with STFF, I realized I needed to stop giving to people who were using me. I was so useful. Being useful only leads to being used. I have a heart to give, and I remember praying to God to help with the gift to give. He turned my heart to the homeless. That's when the STEEL Legacy was born. It took a bit of time before the name arrived, but it was born. You see, I was purposed in this life to be born, to be abused, to withstand, to heal, and to overcome—all so that I could **S**erve, **T**each, **E**ncourage, **E**mpower, and **L**ead. I am the STEEL Legacy.

I care deeply for those who society has labeled unimportant. I will forever extend my time, talents, and resources to those individuals. I am a catalyst for a positive change. So are you! You will need to remember this when you are on your journey to making the world a better place. It is not going to be easy. Entrepreneurship by itself is difficult. Now add fighting wicked problems to that and you have one tough job on your hands. I can tell you, however, it is possible. More so, it is vital work. We need more lightworkers in this world.

"I've been born into a broken world and my purpose is to make sure when I leave it, know I have left my mark of kindness on it somewhere."

—Nikki Rowe, author

This book is going to take you on a journey of my personal story as an Empowered Entrepreneur, specifically in the realm of social entrepreneurship. You will learn more about the STEEL Legacy as we continue, and, because I have a nonprofit side to me, I will be sharing all I know with you regarding that side of the social entrepreneurship house. I have broken this book down into eight different interactive chapters. You will want to do all the call-to-action activities you find along the way, as they will not only help you build a plan of action, but they are designed to incite you from within.

Chapter One will give you a better understanding of what social entrepreneurship really is. You may even already be a social entrepreneur, but I am hopeful you will learn something new. We will cover the following topics:

- Social Entrepreneurship Defined
- The History of Social Entrepreneurship
- The Future of Social Entrepreneurship

Chapter Two will dive deeply into your core. You are the business. You will need to explore who you are, how you see yourself, and what your purpose is. Far too often, we place self-imposed limitations and keep ourselves in bondage. We are going to remove any and all of those limitations and set you free. Let's get you to the next level. Steps are required. You are going to write your IMPACT statement, which will be the foundation of your social entrepreneurship house. We will cover the following topics in Chapter Two:

- Growth Mindset and Grit
- Empathy: The Superpower of All Superpowers
- Researcher

Chapter Three is all about ethics, which is the core of social entrepreneurship. Ethics is one of my favorite topics, and we will have a lot of fun in this section. As a social entrepreneur, you will need to be a very ethical person. How could you be anything else? We will cover the following topics in Chapter Three:

- Ethics as a Life and Legacy
- Power in Doing the Right
- Planet, People, Profit
- Code of Ethics

Chapter Four is set up to give you the fundamentals of entrepreneurship. You will refer to this chapter often. It holds some of the most important information that you will need. Make sure you spend time digesting what you find in this chapter. We will cover the following topics:

- Legal Structures, Including B Corp and Nonprofit
- Business Model Canvas and Pitch Deck
- 4 Types of Intellectual Property

Chapter Five is yet another chapter that you will want to read a few times and will refer to often. Here, your creativity will be tested. I believe you will enjoy the call-to-action actives found in this section. We will cover the following topics in Chapter Five:

- Emotional Intelligence
- Color Psychology
- SAVE Model
- Marketing Plan
- The Power of Building a Brand That Outlasts Time

Chapter Six will be one of the most important, not only in business, but also in your life. It is all about your numbers. Your money. You must get a handle on your money or it will handle you. The wealthy have their own language. I am going to share all I can with you in this book regarding that language. We will cover the following topics:

- Understanding Your Numbers
- Revenue Model
- Start-Up Costs
- Crowdfunding
- Venture Capital and Angel Investors
- Fundraising

Chapter Seven will explore leadership and what it truly means in the context of social entrepreneurship. This is one of the topics I speak on often. I am a leadership expert and in the business of building up leaders. The human economy is a powerful economy. We are going to explore how to benefit, uplift, and empower that economy—starting with yourself. We will cover the following topics in Chapter Seven:

- Transformational Leadership
- Leaders Build Up More Leaders, Not Followers
- The Power of Human Capital, Human Resources, and Volunteers

Chapter Eight will close us out and will be a very touching chapter. I am going to give you all I have as I send you on your way. We will all turn to dust someday. This is why it is important to leave a lasting legacy—one that will continue to make an IMPACT after you are long gone. The call-to-action activities in this chapter might be the most powerful ones you will do. They will be hard. You may even cry. I welcome those tears. They will give you strength that you may not even know you had. We will cover the following topics in Chapter Eight:

- The Goal Is Not to Last Forever but to Build Something That Will
- Breaking of Generational Curses and Planting of Generational Blessings
- Legacy Letter

The way out is within. I am big on critical thinking and making you dig deep. I encourage you to open your mind as much as possible. If you don't think for yourself, someone will think for you. That, in itself, is a matrix. You will hear me mention the matrix often. I reside outside the matrix. I do enter it as often as needed. I look like an agent when I am in there, but I am really a glitch. I am constantly setting people free. I am a modern-day freedom fighter, and if you are ready, you will not only receive the tools you need to become an amazing social entrepreneur, you will also receive access to the escape route of the matrix. Then it will be on you to help as many people as you can. Welcome to *IMPACT!*

Chapter 1
Social Entrepreneurship: The Movement

"Be the change that you wish to see in the world."

—Mahatma Gandhi, activist

We are in the new millennium, and we are seeing a rise in social entrepreneurs. They have always been around. They have been labeled as humanitarians or saints. However, all that is changing. I used to call myself a humanitarian—and yes, I am—but more so, I am a social entrepreneur. Investopedia defines a social entrepreneur as *"a person who pursues novel applications that have the potential to solve community-based problems. These individuals are willing to take on the risk and effort to create positive changes in society through their initiatives."*

You will see as you read this book that social entrepreneurs are similar to business entrepreneurs. You will need all the same tools to build a business fighting social needs that you would need in building a business that is profit only. The biggest difference between the two is that social entrepreneurs are not in pursuit of profit. They are in pursuit of IMPACT. Of course, they may make a profit, but the main motive is to create opportunities, products, services, innovations, and initiatives that will shape the world into a better place.

"Social entrepreneurs are not content just to give a fish or teach how to fish. They will not rest until they have revolutionized the fishing industry."

—Bill Drayton, author of *Leading Social Entrepreneurs Changing the World*

Social entrepreneurs have the commission on their lives to fight the wicked problems of the world. Those problems are large and complex. Many times, there is no clear solution. They are problems such as poverty, environmental, sustainability, equality, education, terrorism, health and wellness, and, the biggest elephant in the room, TRAUMA. The wicked problem I fight the most is homelessness. I have been serving the homeless since 2003. However, I am also a child advocate, and my life's work is dealing with the elephant in the room. I speak openly and publicly about trauma. I study the effects trauma has on the mind and body. You have already seen me address it in this book. My heart is set on helping as many people as possible find healing and freedom with regard to the abuse they have endured and the trauma that keeps them bound.

Homelessness is an epidemic that is deeply tied to mental health. I have seen young, old, and everything in between living on the streets. I have met some of the most fascinating people whose lives were turned upside down. They ended up in situations they never saw coming. Truth is, many of us are just one paycheck away from being without. This is why we should never look down on anyone because we, too, could be in the same place one day.

I am not a for-profit business but rather a nonprofit. For nonprofit, we rely heavily on volunteers and donations to support the work we do. I could not do what I do without both. As I shared before, STEEL Legacy stands for Serve, Teach, Encourage, Empower, and Lead. This is my mission in life. Not just to the homeless, but to all humankind.

STEEL Legacy has an outreach once a quarter. Each quarter is designed to serve a specific need. I am currently working on my summer outreach as I write this book. Summer is dedicated to providing cold water and fresh fruit. Did you know the homeless die due to heat? Well, they do. The goal of the summer outreach is to provide as many people who are homeless with as much cold water as possible. We fill up large storage containers with water and ice and head out to the streets. In addition, we provide fresh fruit, snack food, and whatever food donations we get.

Our fall outreach is dedicated to providing a full meal and rain gear. Anything that can help keep their belongings dry. We collect any and all donations. Many times we receive clothing, which we also take out with us. Our winter outreach is dedicated to helping them keep warm. Just as they can die of heat in the summer, they can also freeze to death in the winter. We provide everything from blankets, coats, sweaters, scarfs, hats, gloves, socks, and the like. We also provide hand warmers, which help tremendously in keeping the body warm, especially if placed on the lower part of the back where our body temperature is regulated. Our spring outreach is dedicated to providing hygiene needs. This outreach requires the most help and donations. We create hygiene bags for both men and women. We do our best to fill them with all they might need for personal care.

Each outreach has some essential items regardless of what season it is. Water is included in every outreach. A first aid kit is always included—some Band-Aids, alcohol swabs, and ointment. If we can help mend a wound on their body, they are less likely to get infections. We always provide some type of food—whether it be a cracker packet, snack food, or some fruit. Each quarter we serve hundreds of people who are homeless. I wish I could say we are serving fewer over the years, but the truth is that we are serving more and more.

I will share more of the journey of the STEEL Legacy as we move forward in the book. For now, I want you to take a moment and just reflect. What is in your heart to fix? What problems do you see in the world that you believe are meant for you to address? We, as social entrepreneurs, have a burning desire in our hearts to address the problems we see. We bring forth social change. Take some time to think and write all that comes to you. Now is your time to put on paper what is in your heart. Don't hold back.

"So never lose an opportunity of urging a practical beginning, however small, for it is wonderful how often in such matters the mustard-seed germinates and roots itself."

—Florence Nightingale, nurse and statistician

Do you know how tiny a mustard seed is? It is one of the tiniest seeds around. Yet, in that tiny seed lies power. When planted, it becomes one of the largest plants in the garden. So big that birds can perch on it for shade and safety. Don't ever underestimate humble beginnings. Just like the mustard seed, you, too, can have an IMPACT in this world by just starting where you are at. This is why I had to write earlier about the problems you see and where your heart burns to help. We can all do our part. We just have to start. I can remember many times when I was doing outreaches that I had little help and not much to give. I would go through my home and find all I could. I would be left with one blanket for myself and one for my son. The others were going to the homeless. I would go through my cabinet and search for food that I could share. I was going to serve regardless if help came or not. I was that mustard seed. I was planted in my purpose. Today, all these years later, my seed has grown tremendously. And the future of my work is bright. The IMPACT I've seen is nothing like it is going to be in the future.

We live in the knowledge of good and evil. Therefore, the need for social entrepreneurs will always exist. We are going to need armies of people whose hearts are not after money, but rather helping humankind prosper, be healed, and empowered. Should you choose to go down the path of social entrepreneurship, you are going to be the catalyst for change. You are going to be creating, designing, implementing, managing, building, and bringing forth change in a broken world. You will need to have the same tools as other entrepreneurs. You will need to understand your work is not going to be easy. Entrepreneurship itself is not for the faint of heart. Social entrepreneurship is even tougher. We, in essence, are fighting the underworld. The corruption. The evil. The unjust. We are the superheroes in the world. Our mission is to have a lasting and profound IMPACT. Our lives save lives. We must never lose hope in our mission and our calling. We are the future, and the future is now.

Chapter 2
The Mind of a Social Entrepreneur

"I truly believe in positive synergy, that your positive mindset gives you a more hopeful outlook, and belief that you can do something great means you will do something great."

—Russell Wilson, American athlete

You would be surprised to know how much our thoughts affect our biology. As I have shared with you, I study trauma—specifically the toll it takes on our mind and body. I am currently considering earning my doctoral degree, and my focus is most likely going to be on intergenerational trauma. Trauma affects our mental health, which has a direct effect on our physical body. There is something called the placebo effect. As defined by the dictionary, the placebo effect *"is a beneficial effect produced by a placebo drug or treatment, which cannot be attributed to the properties of the placebo itself and must therefore be due to the patient's belief in that treatment."* I shared with you in the introduction the statistics regarding our thoughts—how many thoughts per day we have and how research shows the percentage of those thoughts being negative is very high. There is great power in our thoughts. For the placebo effect, it is generally a positive experience. However, negative thoughts create that same effect. Negativity breeds negativity. It usually manifests as aches and illnesses in our bodies and stagnation in our lives. This is what plagues our world.

Entrepreneurs have a particular mind. Though there are other common traits we share, the most common is our mind. We have what is called a growth mindset. There are two types of mindsets: fixed and growth. Carol Dweck, a Stanford psychologist, has done extensive research on the growth mindset.

The fixed mindset is constraining and keeps us bound. The growth mindset, on the other hand, is very liberating. The fixed mindset believes that talent and intelligence are all that's needed to be successful. The fixed mindset doesn't take well to criticism or failure, and normally only sees one way of doing things. The growth mindset believes that talent and intelligence, combined with hard work, will win every time. Even in failure, the growth mindset sees a winning score. The growth mindset is a lifelong learner and never turns down an opportunity to better oneself. The growth mindset understands the importance of practice and being dedicated to pursuing goals. The growth mindset goes through setbacks with an innate ability to persevere. The growth mindset is gritty.

The growth mindset is mission-critical to being successful in entrepreneurship, and, as a social entrepreneur, I believe we need an extra dosage of it because we fight some bigger issues. Not only do we have normal ups and downs in business, but we are fighting wicked problems. The wicked don't always fight fair. We must be a skilled boxer. We must be able to handle blow after blow—knowing that with each punch, we are being shaped into the vision we are in pursuit of. We must not faint when trouble comes and throw in the towel. We need the spirit of Muhamad Ali, the greatest boxer of all time. He would train until he was just about dead, then he would train just a little bit longer. Why? He believed in his fight. He had full confidence that he'd become the greatest boxer of all time. He also understood it wasn't going to happen by standing around. He was going to have to visualize and work for the outcome he wanted to see. He needed to be prepared for the battle. What started in his mind became his reality, but he wasn't afraid to work for it. In order to achieve the greatness he desired, he was going to have to work hard for a long time.

"Impossible is just a big word thrown around by small men who find it easier to live in the world they've been given than to explore the power they have to change it. Impossible is not a fact. It's an opinion. Impossible is not a declaration. It's a dare. Impossible is potential. Impossible is temporary. Impossible is nothing."

—Muhammad Ali, professional boxer and activist

I need you to understand that entrepreneurship requires intense discipline, sacrifice, wisdom, ability to handle setbacks with rigor, and a very high emotional intelligence (EI). Talent will only take you so far, and knowledge must accompany you at every dance you attend. Nothing is impossible. There is no dream or vision that is unachievable. However, your ability to handle the ups and downs of the journey and have the greatest IMPACT will require you to have grit. What is grit, you ask? Grit is passion and perseverance in the face of hardship. It is a sustained effort on the road to achieving your goals. Simply put, grit will not be stopped. It may rest for a bit, but if a person with grit has a set goal, that goal will be accomplished, no matter the obstacles.

I am one gritty person. If I set a goal, I will accomplish it. I am a Lion, and that is what Lions do. Before we close this chapter out, I will introduce you to the four animals. They are going to be the force behind your superpower. All of my students have superpowers. In social entrepreneurship, there is the superpower of all superpowers. Now, it doesn't always feel like a superpower, but I promise it is. What is the superpower of all superpowers? EMPATHY! Yes, you read that right. The dictionary defines empathy as *"the ability to understand and share the feelings of another."* How many of you know you are an empath? A person who feels others' energy and absorbs it? Did you think you were cursed? Well, you are not. You have the greatest superpower around. When combined with the strength of your animals, you are going to be one unstoppable beast.

A study at the University of Michigan revealed that empathy levels in our world have dropped dramatically—*"College kids today are about 40 percent lower in empathy than their counterparts of 20 or 30 years ago."*[1] Why is that? It's because we are living in a virtual world. Technology is a wonderful thing, but it keeps us from truly connecting. People have also become numb to feelings due to the trauma they are carrying. They have learned to suppress feelings, turn off emotions—until they explode, that is—and simply not care for themselves or others. It makes me sad to think about it because of my love for humankind. Humans can be very cruel to one another, but they are the cruelest to themselves. This is how deep the effects of trauma go, and they just spread to future generations. This is why the work I do is so important.

Empathy is a powerful tool to use, and you will need it in business and in life. In my book, *Entrepreneurship Empowered*, I provide a list of what I believe are the four most important talents for entrepreneurs. Insight is one of those talents. Insight is just a fancy word for empathy. You need both empathy and insight with emotional intelligence (EI). The dictionary defines EI as *"the capacity to be aware of, control, and express one's emotions, and to handle interpersonal relationships judiciously and empathetically."* As we explore deeper, you will find that EI is critical in leadership, management, dealing with clients, customer service, human relations, marketing, and so many other aspects of business.

"Clearly, then, the city is not a concrete jungle, it is a human zoo."

—Desmond Morris, author and scientist

Welcome to the jungle. Did you know the world is a jungle? Well, it is, and there are all kinds of animals on the loose. I would like to introduce you to the four of them. There is a Lion, and Lions run this jungle. At least we think we do. We are results-driven. Did you know that a Lion is only awake for four hours of the day? However, what they get done in those four hours is enough to let everyone in the jungle know they are in charge. The same is true with human Lions. We execute and do so at a very high level. What it takes someone else to do in an eight-hour day we finish in four.

The next animal I would like you to meet is the very flashy, ever so beautiful, never shuts up, and doesn't like to be alone, flamingo. They are the hostess with the mostest and will make anyone feel right at home. Very social, the flamingo's strengths are by far its ability to communicate. They make some of the best conversationalists, and you are sure to enjoy the company of a flamingo.

Next, I would like to introduce you to the chameleon. What is the first thing that comes to mind when you think of a chameleon? One of the first things most people think of is that they change color to adapt and fit in. Indeed, the chameleon is one of the best supporters around because they will adapt to their environment. That is until they feel the need to go support someone else. Then they can be called shady—no pun intended. Many times, chameleons are suffering in silence. They struggle with making a decision. They can feel very torn and be pulled at from too many directions. This can make it difficult for them to function. They simply want to see that everyone makes it to shore safely.

The fourth and final animal I would like to introduce you to is the turtle. Everyone needs a turtle on their team. They are the ones with the details. They are going to be cautious and careful with just about everything. They, however, can get in their own way trying to get everything in order. They are slow to execute because they are carefully checking things from all angles. They are the ones that need all the details. They are big on systems and are wonderful planners. However, if something doesn't go according to plan, they can be thrown off.

These are your four animals, and each of them resides in us. We each have them but at different levels. My most dominant animal is the Lion, but coming in at a very close second is my flamingo. I have very little chameleon and almost no turtle, which always cracks me up because I swear I am a details person, and I care for everyone. I do, but then there comes a point where we just have to go regardless if all the pieces are in place or people are ready. Work must be done, and I am expecting to see results.

It is my Lion that has saved me time and time again due to my intense and tragic backstory. I could not have grown my business the way I did without my Lion. I can attest that I move quickly and need to hurry up and slow down. I need to activate turtle power and iron out more details. Slow down. Just wait a few moments longer, then attack. I have never been big on assessments because I am an anomaly, and I can't be put in a box. The 4 Animals is a much different assessment. It tells you your natural side and your adaptable side. We change depending on where we are. I am fascinated by the way we adapt, and why we adapt the way we do. The reason being is I hide. I used to hide a lot. I was hiding because I had been abused for so long that I had no true confidence in the beauty of my authentic self. It was not until I began doing the work required to heal myself that I began to love myself. It took a lot of work to get to where I am today, and I am still working on my healing because I refuse to die with the demons. In this life, you must do the work to heal yourself. I believe in personal development and growth. The 4 Animals Assessment is a tool I used along my journey, and now I share it in all my workshops, classes, and books.

The four animals are the strength in my superpowers. I am learning to master each of them to make me a better leader, educator, servant, friend, and parent. I encourage you to take the assessment, which only takes about five minutes. You get a full report that is extremely valuable, especially with regard to building your résumé and biography. The report contains in-depth information regarding how to effectively communicate with other animals, and how you like to be communicated with as well. This is golden. Just like finding out what your love language is, finding out how you communicate and how you prefer to be spoken to is vital to living a more empowered life. In the back of the book, I have listed my contact for the assessment and the code you can use to receive it at a discounted rate. Make sure you don't pass on the opportunity. The way out is within. The deeper you crawl within and heal, the freer you will become. Life is short. How much time has already been lost? Too much, I say. And that ends now.

I need you to understand how you work and get to know yourself better. I need you to understand agreements that you have—those that are truly yours, and those that have been programmed in you. Yes, every human being has been programmed. I need you to find out your programming, and if you truly agree with all that your programming indicates you are. How we see ourselves is directly related to how we will lead our lives. If you believe that your talents are set in stone, then you will stay stuck. You will keep repeating one hell of a rollercoaster ride by trying to prove yourself over and over again. You stay in the valley of validation when you simply need to walk in the victory of being your authentic self. Stop wasting time by trying to prove how great you are—try to grow and get better. When I work with business owners, I want to see them go from good to great, from great to amazing. Even then, I encourage them to keep growing. I want to see them struggle and go through growing pains. I encourage them to stretch themselves, to go to the ultra-limits of their lives. That is where they become ridiculously amazing. That is how you succeed in business and in life. This is how you make an IMPACT!

We are now going to turn our attention to one of the most important requirements for a social entrepreneur. You are a researcher. You must understand this from the start. You will constantly be researching. You are a life learner. You must never, and I mean never, stay at the surface with your thinking. You are not only a critical thinker, you are an extremely critical thinker. You question everything. I also need to hold ground for your research. Not everyone is going to like your findings, especially because you are fighting the wicked problems of the world. Many people are not going to want to hear the truth. Only a lie requires you believe it. The truth is the truth, regardless if you believe it or not. You cannot wear your feelings on your sleeve. Please also know that some people will not like you, and that is okay. You cannot get caught up in whether someone likes you or not. That can be a problem for empaths, which is why you need to activate your animals. You need the power of your Lion to keep feelings at bay. You are a researcher. You will have great knowledge, and you may be called a know-it-all in a derogatory way. Trust this: there is nothing wrong with being a know-it-all. Hell, all the research should give you knowledge, and you should not be ashamed to use that knowledge. You will never know it all, but there is no shame in expressing the knowledge you do have.

When researching, you will always need to ensure your sources are solid, credible, and reliable. With our technology today, everything can be found on the internet, but that doesn't mean everything found there is correct. The best research you will do will be live research by speaking with people directly. Gathering data and processing that data into tangible findings. Make sure you are always keeping good notes on your research and carefully store your research. You are going to uncover much on your journey, and you will need all the pieces you find along the way. I promise all your hard work will pay off. I need you to be a systematic thinker who is process-proven and results-driven. Then you will be unstoppable.

I am now going to close out this chapter with a few call-to-action activities. This is going to set the stage as we move forward. I am first going to have you do some research. The first thing I want you to research is EMDR therapy and brainspotting therapy. EMDR is the therapy I swear by, and the one that has been the most helpful in my journey of healing and being free. I want you to have it as a resource for yourself and be able to share it with others. We don't build businesses; we build up people, and they build businesses. We, as social entrepreneurs, have the greatest commission on our lives to help as many people as we possibly can. Everyone deals with trauma. There is no shame in your story, no matter what. It is your truth.

The second thing I want you to do is think about yourself. Really dig deep and have a come-to-Jesus moment. What areas in your life do you need to work on? What are your strengths and weaknesses? I also want you to know that if you are hurting at all, you are in a safe place with me and you may reach out to me anytime. This is what I am here for—to help those who are ready to cross over, to be free, to escape a layer of the matrix. I want you to think about how you think. Can you be honest with yourself and acknowledge that you, too, have stinking thinking? The truth is we all do. I want you to write down what comes to you. This is a time of reflection in order to be more prepared for the work ahead.

The third thing I want you to do is research your community, your world. What problems do you see there? What are some of the solutions you think you could come up with to help solve those problems? You may already know what wicked problems you want to address, or what social movement you want to be a part of. That is wonderful. Write it down. Do some research in that area and make note of what you find.

The fourth and final thing you will do for me is a two-part activity. You are going to write your "why" statement (also known as your IMPACT statement). Once that's written down, I want you to create a vision board. I am big on vision boards. As entrepreneurs, we don't predict our future; we create it. As empowered individuals, we do the same. This is how we activate our beliefs. I want you to focus your vision board on the IMPACT you will have in this world. I have provided ample space for you to do all that has been asked of you. If you need more space, then simply pull out some paper and get to work. I encourage you to use a pen or pencil and actually write these activities out. There is so much power when we put pen to paper. Our brain is ignited, and we learn at a much different level. We are activating our neurons, and they are firing away as we write. It helps keep our minds sharp and alert. So, write. Then you can make it fancy if you'd like by typing it up in a Word document. In the back of the book, I have shared my "why" statement, my vision board, and instructions on how to create a vision board. Please use the space provided to do all four of the call-to-action activities.

Chapter 3
Ethics: The Core of Social Entrepreneurship

"In just about every area of society, there's nothing more important than ethics."

—Henry Paulson, author

The very core of social entrepreneurship is ethics. We are fighting the wicked problems of the world, and our moral compass is constantly spinning. We are in pursuit of doing the right thing, and more so doing it on a local and global scale. For a moment, I want you to list all the things that come to mind when you think of ethics, both personally and in business. Use the space provided.

_____
_____
_____
_____
_____

According to the Corporate Finance Institute (CFI), *"Business ethics are the moral principles that act as guidelines for the way a business conducts itself and its transactions. In many ways, the same guidelines that individuals use to conduct themselves in an acceptable way—in personal and professional settings—apply to businesses as well."*

The dictionary defines ethics as *"moral principles that govern a person's behavior or the conducting of an activity."* Ethics includes morals, values, tolerance, and discipline, with all these terms sometimes used interchangeably. According to the book, *How Good People Make Tough Choices: Resolving the Dilemmas of Ethical Living*, Rushworth Kidder writes, *"The core values undergirding ethical thinking are the principles of:*

- *Nonmaleficence—Do no harm*
- *Beneficence—Promote good*
- *Justice—Equality and right, fairness"*[2]

Ethics, however, can be a gray area because it is a place of rights and wrongs. Who is to say what is right and what is wrong? Since we were little, we have been programmed with what is right and what is wrong. This program is shaped by our family, cultures, traditions, heritage, religious affiliation, and so on. *"Be a good girl or good boy,"* I am sure you have heard before. However, there is not always a right way or a wrong way. Have you ever heard the saying, *choosing between two evils?* What about having to choose between two goods? This is an ethical dilemma. The Corporate Finance Institute defines an ethical dilemma as *"a problem in the decision-making process between two possible options, neither of which is absolutely acceptable from an ethical perspective."* Many times in our lives, we will come across ethical dilemmas, and we will just have to choose. The decision you make will be based on a number of different factors, and, depending on how you were raised, your background will play a large part in what decision you make.

In Rushworth Kidder's book, *How Good People Make Tough Choices: Resolving the Dilemmas of Ethical Living*, he suggests that decision-making is driven by our core values, morals, and integrity, and falls into two categories: moral temptations and ethical decisions. Kidder's Four Paradigms for Understanding Ethical Dilemmas are:

1. "***Truth vs. Loyalty****: Truth, for most people, is conformity with facts or reality. Loyalty involves allegiance to a person, corporation or body of people, a government, or set of ideas to which one owes fidelity. It is right to stand on truth. It is right to be loyal.*

2. ***Individual vs. Community****: Individualism assumes that in a society where each person vigorously pursues his own interests, the social good would automatically emerge. As such, the rights of the individual are to be preserved. By 'community' it is meant that the needs of the majority outweigh the interests of the individual. Communities speak to us in a moral voice. They lay claims on their members. It is right to consider the individual. It is right to consider the community.*

3. ***Short-Term vs. Long-Term****: Short-term concerns are usually associated with the satisfaction of current needs in such a way as to preserve the possibility of a future. Long-term concerns are usually defined by the projection of future interests in such a way that there will be ample means to meet future required needs. It is right to think and plan short-term. It is right to think and plan long-term.*

4. ***Justice vs. Mercy****: Justice urges us to stick by our principles, hold to the rules despite the pressures of the moment, and pursue fairness without attention to personalities or situations. Mercy urges us to care for the peculiar needs of individuals case by case and to seek benevolence in every way possible. It is right to be merciful. It is right to enforce justice.*"[2]

I am now going to give you an ethical dilemma case to think about. You must decide what you will do. I have provided space for you to note your decision and why you are making that decision.

"A Doctor's Dilemma: A Case of Two 'Right' Answers," by Abraar Karan: *"Imagine you are a doctor running a clinic in a primarily lower-income neighborhood, where many of your patients are recent immigrants from different parts of the world. You are granted a fixed annual budget of $100,000 through your local public health department. It is unlikely that you can obtain additional funding later in the year. Traditionally, you have used your entire budget for the past several years, which usually lasts from January until December. This allows you to care for all of the few thousand patients who come to you for treatment throughout the year.*

One day in January, a frightened, thin young man appears in the clinic with a folder of medical records. He is accompanied by his aunt, who explains to you that he has recently traveled from El Salvador, where he was diagnosed with a rare type of cancer that, if untreated, will result in his death within six months. After further inquiry, you determine that his cancer is treatable, but will require $50,000 of your budget to save his life. What do you do?"[3]

"Ethics are not necessarily to do with being law-abiding. I am very interested in the moral path, doing the right thing."

—Kate Atkinson

As social entrepreneurs who are going to make a lasting IMPACT in this world, you will be called to be an ethical person and morally correct. You will need to live your life as such. Doing the right thing will always pay off. Even when no one is looking, you will need to do the right thing. That is when it really matters the most. I was not always the most ethical person. I was very poor and lived in a survival mindset. You see, it is the mindset that sets the stage for everything in life. Seeing that my mindset was in survival mode, I did what I needed to do to survive. So, when my manager told me that she would split some cash with me when I delivered pizzas, I took the deal. It was the manager who was in on it. My baby needed diapers. In spite of those choices and behaviors, I never was able to come out of poverty during that time. Taking the deal never made me rich. On the contrary, I stayed poor. And it didn't feel good. It just felt wrong in my soul.

The Greek philosophers, Socrates and Plato, are known for theorizing that we are all born with a soul, which consists of our mind, emotions, and our desires. Within us is our essence. I am big on the saying: *the way out is within*. I truly believe what we need already resides within us. It takes living and experience to help bring it out, but if we are still long enough, and we focus our energy, we can tap into what we already possess. There are other theories that say we were born good, and others that say we were born into sin, imperfect in all our ways. Then there is yet another theory that states we are born neutral—that our moral principles are not already set within us but rather shaped by our cultures. The biggest of those shapers being our parents.

You see how perplexing ethics is? Why we do the things we do is truly based on our programming. Having a deeper understanding of self, as discussed prior, is essential to living the life you are deserving of. The more you can tap into your true authentic self and operate out of it, the freer you become. The more you call off agreements you never agreed to and set in place what you truly do agree to, the stronger you will become. The more you trust yourself and your instincts, the more powerful you will be. There is something to be said about our "gut feeling." Do you listen to your gut? Did you know the gut has a mind? It is often called the second brain. You feel in your gut if something is good or bad. Please pay attention to your gut. This, many times, is your instinct speaking. Animals rely on their instincts to survive. We should rely on ours to thrive.

Live an ethical life. Create a legacy of ethics. Make sure to hold respect for others' beliefs. This doesn't mean you have to agree with them. It just means you respect them and allow them to believe what they believe with no judgment. Discernment is different than judgment. You will need to properly discern situations in your life. However, judgment is not our place. Judgment is based off fear and uses control. Discernment, on the other hand, is the inner voice. It is a truth. Being ethical holds a much higher vibrational level than being unethical. Energy is very real. Make sure you are bringing that energy level into your life by walking in it right.

"I support many organizations that I feel are doing the right thing, like Alonzo Mourning's foundation, Alicia Keys' foundation, the Make-a-Wish Foundation, and other well-established foundations. I kick out a lot of time and money wherever I can."

—Queen Latifah, music artist

There is power in doing the right thing. I know you may see people getting away with murder, but I can promise you all things come to light in due time. There are countless studies that indicate businesses that have a stronger focus on social good and doing right by the people and the planet end up making a much bigger profit. People, planet, and profit is known as the triple bottom line. In business, the bottom line is a term in accounting that tells us what we have made after everything has been taken care of, including taxes. According to Andrew Savitz, principal consultant at Sustainable Business Strategies, the triple bottom line *"captures the essence of sustainability by both measuring the impact of an organization's activities on the world ... including both its shareholder values and its social, human, and environmental capital."*

The social framework is the people. We are going to cover the human capital further along in the book. There is great power in human capital. I want you to research the top companies to work for. What do they offer their employees? What kind of culture do they foster? What are they known for as an employer? You can learn much from these companies and bring those same traits into your business. Taking care of people also means taking care of those who are in the world, too, not just your company. As a social entrepreneur, you will never want to be found using child labor. That would not work at all. You are working to protect those children. You genuinely care for the human, and that is to be commended, especially because we live in a world where humans are often tossed to the wayside with no regard.

The planet is next on the list of Ps. Taking care of our environment is so important. Companies that strive to set sustainable environmental practices in place do much better in business. One of the biggest practices you may hear about is reducing the carbon footprint. This means releasing less waste in the environment. Oftentimes, environmental sustainability is the more profitable course for a business in the long run. Arguments that it costs more to be environmentally sound are often debunked when the course of the business is analyzed over a period of time. Understand that in business, you are in the long game. Yes, it may cost you more up front to be a more environmentally friendly business, but in the long term, it will benefit you greatly.

Furthermore, you will be contributing to the wellness of the world.

Profit is the final P. According to Market Business News, "*Profit is equal to the sale of a product minus all these operating and other expenses, (i.e., fixed costs, variable costs, and taxes). When calculating a business' profits, you must also account for overhead costs. Overhead costs include fixed costs, (i.e., periodic costs that remain the same, such as salaries, rent, and insurance). They also include variable costs (i.e., costs that fluctuate with output, such as labor and materials).*" There is a theory by Adam Smith, who is known as the father of economics, called the invisible hand theory. This theory touches on the unintended benefits of an individual's self-interested actions. For example, a farmer creates a business for his personal gain but contributes to society as a whole by creating jobs and providing food to the community.

The invisible hand theory indicates that there is social good being met, which, by many rights, is not intentional. As a social entrepreneur, you will be intentional. You will be seeking to make an IMPACT. You will be creating a business that will generate profit, but it will not be profit-driven. You will hold true to your core mission, and that is what will lead the way. You may solve problems with people and make improvements for humanity. You may find solutions that work to save the environment, which will also have an impact on humanity. At your core, however, will be a drive to uphold what you believe to be right. You will be using your moral compass to help navigate yourself in the murky waters of the underworld. You will make an IMPACT.

"The only way to truly be protected at all times is to claim your personal power with the highest code of ethics and responsibility. If you are centered in this type of power, the power of the universe supports you, and no one and nothing can defeat you."

—Christopher Penczak, author

The last point I am going to leave you with in this chapter is the code of ethics. Investopedia defines a code of ethics as *"a guide of principles designed to help professionals conduct business honestly and with integrity. A code of ethics document may outline the mission and values of the business or organization, how professionals are supposed to approach problems, the ethical principles based on the organization's core values, and the standards to which the professional is held."* Right now, I want you to take time to develop a personal code of ethics. I want you to reflect on who you are. Take an account of your life. Who are you? If you were to ask a friend to describe you, what do you believe they would say? Write all that comes to you. Then I want you to think about your personal ethics. Make a list of everything that comes to you regarding your ethical beliefs.

Then I want you to think about your personal and work relationships. Are they healthy? Are there things you would like to see change? Is there too much toxic behavior? Do you gossip, or is there too much gossip around you? Just think, could your relationships improve? Again, write everything that comes to you. The next thing I want you to do is write down your top ten values. You can google a list of values that you can look at for reference if you have a hard time coming up with a list. Sometimes if you see a list of words, you can see which one resonates with you. From those ten values, I want you to circle five. From the five you circled, I want you to star the top three. Out of those three, I want you to choose one. This is the one you will never compromise. I want you to write an oath to yourself that you will uphold that value. Then I want you to create a code of ethics. It shouldn't be too difficult to do once you have it all on paper and you know what your top value is.

The first part of the code will be your purpose. You created a "why" statement in the last chapter—you could use that as a starting place for your purpose. Or come up with something new. The second part of the code will be your aspirations, your "I will" statements. Finally, the third part is the beliefs you have. As of a result of your "I will" statements, what do you believe? Remember that you were created for a purpose, and there is a great calling on your life to not only serve humankind, but to make a lasting IMPACT in this world. As a social entrepreneur, you will live by your code of ethics. Now is your time to develop what that is going be. Really take time for this activity.

_____
_____
_____
_____
_____
_____
_____
_____
_____
_____
_____
_____
_____
_____
_____
_____
_____
_____
_____
_____
_____
_____
_____
_____
_____

Chapter 4
Legal Structures, Intellectual Property, and Business Planning

"I always wondered if there was a purpose to the universe, if there was a plan, if there was some sort of organizing factor, hopefully that I played a role in."

—John Green, author

As social entrepreneurs, you do play a role in the plan of the universe. You are going to make an IMPACT. You are creating a legacy that will outlast you and live beyond. This, at least, is the pursuit of a social entrepreneur. The information covered in this chapter and the chapters ahead will be very important to you as you begin to structure and organize your business. I strongly encourage you to read these chapters over a few times to fully digest them. I also encourage you to highlight and make notes along the way. The many terms and definitions shared in this chapter are common in business. I, however, will dive deeper with regard to nonprofit and B Corp, as those are for social entrepreneurship endeavors, but you can structure your business using any of the options provided. It is up to you.

After I take you through how to legally structure your business, I am going to share with you the four different types of intellectual property. Many of you will create products and services that you will want to protect. We all have intellectual property. It is important that you take the necessary steps to protect your intellectual property so that no one else takes it and runs with it. Once we cover that, I will close the chapter on business planning and share with you the truth about the traditional business plan. I will expose you to a more modern-day way of planning. There are several call-to-action activities in this chapter. Make sure to do them all.

Business Legal Structures

The way you legally structure your business is an important step, and far too often, it's done quickly or even overlooked. I have many a story of students and clients who didn't do the research needed to make such an important business decision. They ran right into a Limited Liability Company (LLC) because they saw that other businesses were formed that way, so it must be the best way. LLCs have been buzzing for some years now. However, an LLC is not for everyone. Far too many people structure their business that way without asking the important questions and really looking at their business. They then spend more money than needed, end up with a business legal structure not suited for them, and a loss at the end of the year. Please take the time to make the best decision for your business, and don't just go with what everyone else is doing. I need you to think critically about how you are going to structure your business.

The first step in structuring your business is to assess your risks. What are they? You will have both personal and business risks and assets. Could insurance cover those risks? Do you need to be an LLC or corporation to get a contract or do a particular type of work? Some industries may require you to be legally structured as an LLC or corporation. Some may just need you to have insurance and licensing, and that is enough. When choosing your business structure, it is wise to consult with a business lawyer or even a tax accountant. Both will help you make a sound decision.

Sole Proprietorship is the simplest, most inexpensive, and most common business structure. Sole means one owner. Being that the man who owned my business prior was a sole proprietor, I naturally became one as well. As a sole proprietor, I have no protection. The liability is all mine. That is the most important takeaway for sole proprietorship: you are not protected. Of course, there is insurance to acquire, and we will discuss the different types of insurance a little later in the book.

According to the Small Business Administration (SBA), *"sole proprietorships do not produce a separate business entity. This means your business assets and liabilities are not separate from your personal assets and liabilities. You can be held personally liable for the debts and obligations of the business."*[4] Just because you begin as a sole proprietor doesn't mean you will stay one. Amazon is a perfect example of a company that started as a sole proprietorship, and now Amazon is ruling the world! Okay, so it's not ruling the world, but it is now a publicly traded corporation.

A sole proprietorship is extremely easy to form. In many areas, there is no legal filing fee at all to be a sole proprietor. If you choose to use a business name, you will need to research your local county's process to file for a DBA, also known as **D**oing **B**usiness **A**s. Your DBA becomes your legal name, and then you are able to open a business bank account. My DBA is Start To Finish Files. Having a DBA is very important as well. It adds to your professionalism. This doesn't mean you cannot use your name—many people do. The decision is up to you and what works best for your business. Your business may fall in an area or industry that requires licenses or permits. In that case, you will have a small fee to pay, and you will need to make sure to keep up with the renewal of those licenses and permits so you don't incur additional charges.

Taxes for a sole proprietorship are very simple as well. They are seen as personal taxes. Remember, you and your business are one entity, which means you are together. You will file one tax return, which will lay out your expenses and your income. There is a very lovely self-employment tax that you need to be aware of—it is fairly large, and when you first encounter it, it may shock you. You will want to visit the Internal Revenue Service's website and explore the detailed information regarding taxation for a sole proprietorship. It has a lot of helpful information for you. After all, they are the ones you are paying the money to.

Partnerships are another way many businesses are structured. Partnerships are two or more people who share in the building of a business. Partnerships are an interesting dance, like the two-step; however, not everyone can do the two-step, nor should they try. Understanding yourself is key in knowing whether or not a partnership will work for you. I am a controller, so most partnerships do not work for me. I simply need to be in control, and I must be able to call the shots. I am very comfortable raising people up to lead, as that is part of the business I am in. However, I need them to go lead on another ship, not mine. They come to me to be trained, and I send them out to lead and train others.

Have you ever heard of a "silent partner"? Silent partners are found in **limited partnerships** (LP). According to the SBA, "*Limited partnerships have only one general partner with unlimited liability, and all other partners have limited liability. The partners with limited liability also tend to have limited control over the company, which is documented in a partnership agreement. Profits are passed through to personal tax returns, and the general partner— the partner without limited liability—must also pay self-employment taxes.*"[4] In this type of partnership, the general partner will control all day-to-day managing parts of the business and has full control in that area. The limited partner does not have any managing rights to the business and cannot make any decisions. They are only in their investment, and that is it.

Setting up a partnership is simple. You don't even need a contract, but I highly recommend that you do have a contract to protect yourself. It must be detailed, and it must hold all relevant information, such as who will be doing what (roles), who will make decisions, who will handle the money, who gets what cut of the money, who will hold the most liability, and how will the business dissolve. There are many templates out there regarding partnership contracts. My advice is to research them and find one that works best for you and your partner(s). You can always edit a template to make it yours. You should also consider taking the document to a lawyer for review or even have them create one for you. What you don't want to do is go into business with someone, regardless of how much you trust or love them, without a written contract in hand.

You can also set up your partnership as a **Limited liability partnership (LLP)**. According to the SBA, *"limited liability partnerships are similar to limited partnerships but give limited liability to every owner. An LLP protects each partner from debts against the partnership, and they won't be responsible for the actions of other partners."*[4] This is a much stronger way of setting up your business than using a signed contract. This actually holds protection to the business for liabilities.

As a final reminder regarding partnerships, you are getting into bed with someone, as they say. Be very cautious. Cover your bases. Make sure everything is in writing and that you have a very clear escape clause. Seek legal counsel. Then go roll around in the hay and see if you can make some magic. With partners, we are stronger. We have combined resources, talents, skills, and abilities. Partnerships are known to have nice business lifespans. When done right, partnerships are the stones on which to build a very secure and stable foundation. Two are greater than one, for they have double the labor. Additionally, if either fall, the other is there to pick him or her up.

Now let's turn our attention to this LLC I have been addressing. I am not a big fan of the LLC only because I see far too many people jump into them without really assessing their risks, and they don't need the damn thing. They don't own a house. They are barely in business. They don't have a product or service that holds any risk. They haven't even made it to the market yet. What do you really need protection from? Please think carefully before you jump into an LLC or a corporation. According to the SBA website, "*an LLC lets you take advantage of the benefits of both the corporation and partnership business structures. LLCs protect you from personal liability in most instances, your personal assets—like your vehicle, house, and savings accounts—won't be at risk in case your LLC faces bankruptcy or lawsuits. Profits and losses can get passed through to your personal income without facing corporate taxes. However, members of an LLC are considered self-employed and must pay self-employment tax contributions towards Medicare and Social Security.*

LLCs can have a limited life in many states. When a member joins or leaves an LLC, some states may require the LLC to be dissolved and re-formed with new membership—unless there's already an agreement in place within the LLC for buying, selling, and transferring ownership.

LLCs can be a good choice for medium- or higher-risk businesses, owners with significant personal assets they want to be protected, and owners who want to pay a lower tax rate than they would with a corporation."[4] There are several steps you will need to take to form your LLC. In the back of the book, I have provided what those steps could be. Each state is a bit different in what they require and what the costs are to form your business as an LLC. However, the steps provided will be a good general rule of thumb to follow and prepare for if you do plan to choose an LLC as your business structure.

Before I close the door on LLCs and move on to corporations, I am going to share one more LLC with you because this type of LLC is specific to social entrepreneurs.

You may or may not have heard of it before. It is called a *Low-Profit Limited Liability Company*, also known as **L3C**, and it is defined as *"a legal form of business entity in the United States that was created to bridge the gap between non-profit and for-profit investing by providing a structure that facilitates investments in socially beneficial, for-profit ventures by simplifying compliance with Internal Revenue Service rules for program-related investments, a type of investment that private foundations are allowed to make. An L3C is a for-profit, social enterprise venture that has a stated goal of performing a socially beneficial purpose, not maximizing income. It is a hybrid structure that combines the legal and tax flexibility of a traditional LLC, the social benefits of a nonprofit organization, and the branding and market positioning advantages of a social enterprise. The L3C is obligated to be mission-driven so there is a clear order of priorities for its fiduciaries. The L3C is designed to make it easier for socially oriented businesses to attract investments from foundations and additional money from private investors."*

There are currently only ten states you can form an L3C in. I reside in California, as most of my students and clients do, so, for us, the L3C is not available. The ten states where L3Cs are active:

1. Illinois
2. Michigan
3. North Dakota
4. Kansas
5. Louisiana
6. Maine
7. Rhode Island
8. Utah
9. Vermont
10. Wyoming

The first L3C in the U.S. was formed in 2008, so as you can see, this is a very new legal structure. I am sure it will grow to all states. In order to legally structure your business as an L3C, you must meet the requirements of a program-related investment. On the IRS website is more information regarding such requirements. When you do your research, make sure to search the term L3C along with program-related investments, both of which can be found on the IRS website.

The following information comes directly from the SBA: **Corporation C corp.** *"A corporation, sometimes called a C corp, is a legal entity that's separate from its owners. Corporations can make a profit, be taxed, and can be held legally liable. Corporations offer the strongest protection to their owners from personal liability, but the cost to form a corporation is higher than other structures. Corporations also require more extensive record-keeping, operational processes, and reporting. Unlike sole proprietors, partnerships, and LLCs, corporations pay income tax on their profits. In some cases, corporate profits are taxed twice—first, when the company makes a profit, and again when dividends are paid to shareholders on their personal tax returns. Corporations have a completely independent life separate from their shareholders. If a shareholder leaves the company or sells his or her shares, the C corp can continue doing business relatively undisturbed. Corporations have an advantage when it comes to raising capital because they can raise funds through the sale of stock, which can also be a benefit in attracting employees. Corporations can be a good choice for medium- to higher-risk businesses, or businesses that need to raise money, and businesses that plan to 'go public' or eventually to be sold.*

S corp. *An S corporation, sometimes called an S corp, is a special type of corporation that's designed to avoid the double taxation drawback of regular C corps. S corps allow profits, and some losses, to be passed through directly to owners' personal income without ever being subject to corporate tax rates. Not all states tax S corps equally, but most recognize them the same way the federal government does and taxes the shareholders accordingly. Some states tax S corps on profits above a specified limit and other states don't recognize the S corp election at all, simply treating the* business as a C corp. S corps must file with the IRS to get S corp status, a different process from registering with their state. There are special limits on S corps. S corps can't have more than 100 shareholders, and all shareholders must be U.S. citizens. You'll still have to follow the strict filing and operational processes of a C corp. S corps also have an independent life, just like C corps. If a shareholder leaves the company or sells his or her shares, the S corp can continue doing business relatively undisturbed. S corps can be a good choice for a business that would otherwise be a C corp, but meet the criteria to file as an S corp.

B corp. A benefit corporation, sometimes called a B corp, is a for-profit corporation recognized in the majority of U.S. states. B corps are different from C corps in purpose, accountability, and transparency, but aren't different in how they're taxed. B corps are driven by both mission and profit. Shareholders hold the company accountable to produce some sort of public benefit in addition to a financial profit. Some states require B corps to submit annual benefit reports that demonstrate their contribution to the public good. There are several third-party B corp certification services, but none are required for a company to be legally considered a B corp in a state where the legal status is available.

Close corporation. Close corporations resemble B corps but have a less traditional corporate structure. These shed many formalities that typically govern corporations and apply to smaller companies. State rules vary, but shares are usually barred from public trading. Close corporations can be run by a small group of shareholders without a board of directors.

Nonprofit corporation. Nonprofit corporations are organized to do charity, education, religious, literary, or scientific work. Because their work benefits the public, nonprofits can receive tax-exempt status, meaning they don't pay state or federal taxes income taxes on any profits they make. Nonprofits must file with the IRS to get tax exemption, a different process from registering with their state. Nonprofit corporations need to follow organizational rules very similar to a regular C corp. They also need to follow special rules about what they do with any profits they earn. For example, they can't distribute profits to members or political campaigns. Nonprofits are often called 501(c)(3) corporations—a reference to the section of the Internal Revenue Code that is most commonly used to grant tax-exempt status."[4]

Is your head spinning? Are you perplexed as to which business legal structure to choose? The last few we covered are more specific for social entrepreneurs, so you may want to focus your research on those to start. I have provided all the terms and definitions for each of the structures in the back of the book, along with a chart to better explain. I want you to know the best place to start is as a sole proprietor. You can build up from there. I highly recommend seeking legal counsel. If you are not able to afford a lawyer, I would recommend looking for a local law school. Many times, they have free law clinics.

The students, in my opinion, are fresher than some lawyers, and they are more eager to learn. See what advice they offer you. Deciding your legal structure is important, and you really do need to make the best decision. As I stated in the beginning, you will need to assess your risks and how much you have in assets that could be lost if some legal matter does come up.

You are able to change your business structure along the way, so if starting as a sole proprietor is the wisest choice, then go with it. Then, as you grow in assets or your business grows in risk, you will be able to restructure your business. What I don't want you to do is jump into an LLC, pay large sums of money, and end up on the losing side. On account of business structure being so perplexing, I have provided a chart that lays out all the different types of business structures we have now reviewed. I am also providing some space for you to do some research and just spend a little time thinking about what might be the best way for you to form your business. Do your own research and see what you come up with. Use the space provided to note your findings.

Intellectual Property

"Intellectual property is a key aspect for economic development."

—Craig Venter, scientist

Each of us has intellectual property (IP). IP is an asset to an individual, and many businesses thrive off of IP. I remember all too well my state job interview. In the third and final interview, I politely stated that I had intellectual property available for lease. The interviewers looked at each other and then looked at me. I am not exactly sure what their thoughts were, but I received a call no sooner than I made it home, telling me I was hired and that I started on the Tuesday following the Labor Day holiday. Boom! I was in, just like that. IP sealed the deal. I gave the state quite a bit of my IP until enough was enough. Now I am very protective of my IP, and you should be as well.

There are four major types of IP:

- *"A **copyright** gives the creator of an original work exclusive rights to it, usually for a limited time. Copyright may apply to a wide range of creative, intellectual, or artistic forms, or works. Copyright does not cover ideas and information themselves, only the form or manner in which they are expressed. The life of a copyright lasts the lifetime of the artist/author's life plus 70 years.*
- *A **trademark** is a recognizable sign, design or expression which distinguishes products or services of a particular trader from the similar products or services of other traders. Trademarks last 10 years and are able to be renewed every 10 years.*
- *A **trade secret** is a formula, practice, process, design, instrument, pattern, or compilation of information, which is not generally known or reasonably ascertainable, by which a business can obtain an economic advantage over competitors and customers. There is no formal government protection granted;*

> *each business must take measures to guard its own trade secrets (e.g., Formula of its soft drinks is a trade secret for Coca-Cola.)*
> - *A **patent** is a form of right granted by the government to an inventor or their successor-in-title, giving the owner the right to exclude others from making, using, selling, offering to sell, and importing an invention for a limited period of time, in exchange for the public disclosure of the invention. An invention is a solution to a specific technological problem, which may be a product or a process and generally has to fulfill three main requirements: it has to be new, not obvious and there needs to be an industrial applicability. The patent will have a life span of 20 years from the filing date."*

As social entrepreneurs, we are serious about fixing the problems we see in our world. It is highly likely you will create a product or service that needs to be protected in one of the forms of IP given. There are really important things to remember when working with your IP. Don't tell just anyone. If you believe you have an idea for a product that can be patented, then I need you to go do a patent search. I want you to give it a try right here in this chapter. Just so you can see all the different patents that are out there. You can do a patent search on something you love or use daily. Then you can search around for some ideas you have had and see if they have been patented.

I can remember my uncle having an idea regarding a motorcycle helmet that had a brake light in the back of the helmet. His thought was brilliant. We see the back of the head of the rider more than we do that small brake light at the top of the seat. Why wouldn't we want to create such an item? Well, after a patent search, wouldn't you know it, we found a patent for that same concept. What's interesting is I have never personally seen such a helmet on the market. At any rate, there was a patent for it. One thing I need you to remember before I send you off to research is that there is a cost involved in protecting your IP. It will be worth every penny if you are sitting on a product or service that hits the mass market for takeover. You definitely want to hire an attorney who works specifically with IP. Do not risk going to one who doesn't—you may end up not just losing your IP, but a lot of money, too.

On the space provided, I want you to go now and do some research on patents and trademarks. You will find the patent and trademark search on the same website: https://www.uspto.gov/. You will go to that website and start with a patent search. Then you will do a trademark search. I also encourage you to read over the information on the site. Explore the site, not just the search option.

Business Plans

We are now going to turn our attention to business plans. I indicated early on in this book that I was going to expose the truth of business, and that is exactly what I am going to do. I am not a big believer in the business plan. I very much believe in planning, and I plan all the time. However, planning without doing is like wishing without working. You cannot just wish your way through life, nor can you just plan your way through it, either. You must work. You must take your plan and your wish and get to work so you are prepared for what you have asked for.

"Unless you are a fortune-teller, long-term business planning is a fantasy."

—Jason Fried, co-founder of 37signals

I myself never started with a business plan. The only time I ever wrote a business plan was when I earned my master's degree. My final project was to write a business plan. The plan I wrote was for a nonprofit after school arts program in underprivileged communities. I cannot for the life of me tell you where that plan is. I never used it. Business plans are overrated. Planning is not. If you were under the impression you needed to write a business plan to start a business, I am here to burst that bubble. Many people do write plans, but they only collect dust on a shelf somewhere, or they are tucked in a drawer and never come out. There are certainly reasons for writing a business plan. One of the biggest reasons is to get funding. Somewhere along the line, you will likely want to get a business loan or seek out an investor.

The Small Business Administration (SBA) backs 80% of small business loans. They are not the ones that give the loans out; they only back the loan. The banks loan the money to the lender. You must be credit-worthy in order to receive a loan. Please keep in mind, even existing businesses that have been in business for many years and have solid statistical data can be disqualified by the SBA. Your chances are much higher if you have excellent credit, and your personal and business finances are in good health. *"The SBA requires a personal guarantee from every owner with at least a 20% ownership stake and from others who hold top management positions. A personal guarantee puts you and your personal assets on the hook for payments if your business can't make them."*[4] I encourage you to go to the SBA's website, www.sba.gov, and explore. It is one of your most valuable resources and has a never-ending wealth of information. They will show you a traditional business plan, and now they even have one that is a lean version.

The traditional business plan is 28 to 35 pages in length, plus appendices that include financial statements. The business plan is a series of several different types of analysis. It will have a cover page where the name of the business, the owner's name, and their contact information can be found. The next thing the reader sees is the table of contents. Business plans are lengthy. The table of contents helps the reader navigate the space. The executive summary is crucial to the business plan and is found directly after the table of contents. In the back of the book, I have provided a template of what a traditional business plan consists of.

My advice to you is that you seek out help when writing your plan. You will never take one class or go to a one-time workshop and come out some badass business plan writer. That is just not going to happen. It takes a lot of work to write a well-written business plan. And, in order to receive funding, you will need one that is well done. Therefore, I recommend you find someone who has been writing them and can help you. Your chances of getting funded are much higher with a well-written plan and solid data. To write or not to write a business plan is really up to you. Remember that if you are seeking a bank loan, you will most definitely need to write a business plan. If you are starting a business, however, you have other options available to you. We are now going to explore those options. I believe you will be pleasantly surprised to see how much more efficient and effective these more modern ways of planning are.

"It's amazing how many professional possibilities appear when you use value and purpose—rather than skills—as the starting point for reinventing your career."

—Alexander Osterwalder, author, speaker, and entrepreneur

Alexander Osterwalder developed the business model canvas. I love the business model canvas so much. It is perfect for a business at any stage. The business model canvas is your new best friend. It starts as a business model, which has four key drivers: the offering, the customers, the infrastructure, and the financial viability.

INFRASTRUCTURE	OFFERING	CUSTOMERS
FINANCES		

Those four key drivers then expand into nine building blocks. Those nine building blocks are the foundation for building a solid plan for your business.

What you will see in the next illustration is that the offering is the only thing that doesn't break down. The reason for this is that the offering is your "purple cow"—it is your value proposition statement. It is what sets you apart from all others. Your infrastructure will break down into three drivers: key partners, key activities, and key resources. Your customers will break down into three drivers as well: customer relationship, customer channels, and customer segments. The base of your model—finances—is broken in half: cost structure and revenue structure.

Key Partners	Key Activities	Value Proposition	Customer Relationships	Customer Segments
	Key Resources		Channels	
Cost Structure		Revenue Streams		

Both images were created by IMPACT based on Alexander Osterwalder, Business Model Generation

The offering, which is also called the value proposition and or customer value proposition (CVP), is, in many respects, the most important part of your business model. Your job is to provide the most value you can to your customers/clients and the market you serve. You should be offering better value than your competitors, and you should be able to have sustainability, meaning you must be able to execute on your value for a length of time. The value proposition solves problems and relieves pain. As social entrepreneurs, this is our starting point. We see the problems in the world that we know we can help address either by creating a product or service specific to the issues we have identified as our fight. I am now going to have you take some time to work on your business model canvas. You will start with your CVP. Then you will work through the remaining parts. This is just to get your thoughts out on paper. Don't hold back, and don't hold too tightly to anything. This is all drafting. Then you will tighten up to form a more formal plan. For your CVP, there are three questions to ask yourself:

- *What is the issue I am solving?*
- *Why would someone want to have this issue solved?*
- *What is the underlying motivator for this issue?*

Take a moment now and ask yourself those questions and write down what comes to you.

Customer segments: Who are your customers? Who are the most important customers? The more detailed you can be with your customer segment, the better you will be able to market to them.

Channels: How are you going to communicate, distribute, and sell to your customers? Which way do they prefer? What are the most cost-effective channels? What are the most time-effective channels?

Customer relations: What way(s) will you get and keep new customers? How does this strategy fit in with the other parts of the business model?

Key resources: What do you need in order to offer your CVP?

Key activities: What will you need to do in order to provide your CVP?

Key partnerships: Who all will you need in order to deliver on your CVP? Who are your partners and suppliers? What things will you need to outsource to your partners? What resources do you need from your partners? Who is on your team?

Cost structure: What are all of your costs involved in operating and running your business to fulfill your CVP?

Revenue streams: What are your customers willing to pay? What do they currently pay for solving the problem? How many different revenue streams do you potentially have?

I am a realist. I don't believe that making a student write a business plan in college is the way to truly teach the student. I believe in doing pieces of the plan, and even more so, in using the business model canvas as a starting point. Many college students don't have an existing business, so to have them develop a business plan is a waste of time. What is more relevant is for them to learn pieces of the plan that are important, such as company profile, products and services offered, pricing structure, competencies in computer analysis, marketing, and, of course, financial viability. Then being able to take that information and present it to investors or banks for loans. Presenting is critical.

The social-emotional learning piece is more important to me than the writing piece. Not to say that I don't wish to see my students learn how to write—I certainly do. But what I don't want is for them to be able to write a paper and not be able to speak their plan. The power of life and death is in the tongue. I've said it before, and I'll say it again: Speak your truth. Speak your vision. Speak life.

A pitch deck is a slide presentation that, many times, is built off of by using the canvas model. It will clearly tell your target audience the key essentials of your business. More importantly, it starts by addressing what the problem is and what solution you have that fixes the problem. There are many templates out there to use. Guy Kawasaki is very well-known for pitch decks and has several templates to review and use. Right now, stop reading and search "Guy Kawasaki pitch decks." You are looking for the top ten slides you need for your pitch deck, according to Guy. I want you to then write those ten slides in the space provided below. Also, be sure to note any other suggestions he has for you regarding the presentation. Then explore the templates he provides, and make sure to save a few for future reference.

The pitch deck is a tool you will use to present as you speak your vision. I am sure you were surprised to read that not one Fortune 500 company wrote a business plan. You may also be shocked to learn how powerful the pitch deck tool is, and how many businesses use it to enter the market and receive funding. Businesses such as LinkedIn, Airbnb, and Square have all used a pitch deck, and it has been a big key to their success. My confidence is that it will be just as useful to you in your journey as you create your business, which I know will make an IMPACT. Remember that you must put your words into action, or they will die right along with you. The way you create something that outlasts you is to make sure you get up and do it. You cannot dream forever; you cannot plan forever. You must get up and run the race. You must lift your wings and take flight.

Chapter 5
Marketing and Branding

"You can never go wrong by investing in communities and the human beings within them."

—Pam Moore, CEO of Marketing Nutz

I love marketing and branding. I could write an entire book on those two subjects. Maybe one day, I will. For now, I will just give you as much as I can in this chapter. I will start by letting you know right now that emotional intelligence and marketing go hand in hand. Emotional intelligence allows us to understand the customer or client better. Brands such as Procter and Gamble, Coca-Cola, and Nike are brilliant at using emotional intelligence in their marketing strategies. There are many studies that indicate how these brands used emotional intelligence in commercials, and, in return, commercial sales grew. When we tap into the emotions of our fellow human beings, we tap into a goldmine. People are often driven by emotion. We love to feel. When we use emotional intelligence, we can empathize with them. We, too, can feel their pain or their joy. When this takes place, we can come up with better solutions to problems. As social entrepreneurs, this is key. We are some of the biggest problem solvers the world will ever see.

Your greatest marketing tool is word of mouth (WOM). This, too, is tied to emotional intelligence. You must be able to connect and relate to your customers and clients. Even more importantly, you must be making sure the job they need you to do is being done properly and in such a way that they have to tell everyone they know all about you and your business. How do you build successful WOM marketing? You start with a foundation made of solid trust, commitment, and customer satisfaction. You make sure your customers or clients have some of your swag. T-shirts, coffee cups, pens, notepads—anything you can give to them to use that showcases your brand. Another way is to give a referral discount for sending new customers or clients your way. *"Bring a new customer and receive a percentage off your next order!"* Or better yet, give something away for FREE for the referral. According to Jonah Berger's bestselling book, *Contagious: Why Things Catch On*, there are six key factors that drive what people talk about and share. They are organized in an acronym called STEPPS, which stands for:

- "*Social Currency*—the better something makes people look, the more likely they will be to share it
- *Triggers*—things that are top of mind (i.e., accessible) are more likely to be tip of tongue
- *Emotion*—when we care, we share. High-arousal emotions increase sharing
- *Public*—the easier something is to see, the more likely people are to imitate it
- *Practical Value*—people share useful information to help others
- *Stories*—Trojan Horse stories carry messages and ideas along for the ride"[5]

"Color is a power which directly influences the soul."

—Wassily Kandinsky

Let's now connect some more marketing dots by adding a little color. I am completely fascinated by the mind. Why we do what we do and how we tick. Being on this path of enlightenment, I have also encountered the power of color psychology and how to use it in my own marketing and branding. Did you know that colors have meanings and make us feel a certain way? We may not even realize it in our conscious mind, but our subconscious certainly does.

According to colorpsycology.org, *"Color psychology is a well-known, yet less explored branch of the study of how our brain perceives what it visualizes. As far as scientific research goes, there is not much to work with. However, the impact that colors have on our brains is used to manipulate our decision making by multiple facets of society."*[6] Influencing decision-making is an important key in marketing. As marketers, we are creating a message that will prompt you to buy or use services. My signature color is blue. Here is what blue is known for:

- Unique and authentic
- Enthusiastic, sympathetic, and personal; they seek meaning and significance in life
- Warm, communicative, and compassionate; they care about what they do
- Idealistic, spiritual, and sincere; they value unity and integrity in their relationships
- Peaceful, flexible, and imaginative; they are natural romantics and nurturers

Sounds just like me and everything I represent. It is my personal brand, as well as my business brand color. Your personal brand is the base of your business brand, and we will explore personal brand a little later in the chapter.

I would like for you to do a little research on color psychology. Before you do the research, start by writing down some of your favorite colors and what colors you think you would use for your brand. Then, when you explore the website given, make sure to write down the meaning to those colors. After you know the meaning, will you stay with those colors as part of your brand, or will you change them?

You are now going to start building your brand by using the colors chosen in your marketing and advertisements. https://www.colorpsychology.org/color-psychology-marketing/.[6]

"The best marketing strategy ever: CARE."

—Gary Vaynerchuk, entrepreneur, speaker, and marketing expert

As social entrepreneurs, we care deeply. This is what keeps us going and empowers us to fight the good fight. This will always be in our marketing strategy. Our strategy will have many parts to it. We have already covered the importance of emotional intelligence, creating a buzz with WOM, and color psychology. That is the groundwork. Now we are going to turn our attention to the basic principle found in marketing and what is called the marketing mix. I, however, am going to share a new model to the marketing mix, which I believe is a better fit for us as social entrepreneurs. The marketing mix is also known as the 4 Ps: *Product, Price, Promotion, and Place*. It has been used in marketing for a very long time. Studies show that it puts too much focus on the product and not enough on why the customer would need it. The 4 Ps have been reshaped into a more effective marketing model. The **S.A.V.E** model: **S**olution *(Product),* **A**ccess *(Place),* **V**alue *(Price),* and **E**ducation *(Promotion).* As social entrepreneurs, we are creating products or services that provide a solution. Therefore, I truly believe this model is better suited for us and it's one that I will encourage you to use as you build your marketing plan. I want you to understand that your product or service is the solution. My slogan for STFF for many years has been: *"The Better Solution."* This saying is my personal mantra, as well. There is always a better solution. Period. Do not get all caught up in the features of your product or service; instead, get caught up in solving the problem for your customers. You are there to meet their needs—remember that.

How easily accessible your business is to your target market is so very important. This is why online retail is booming. The access to get what we need when we need it is one click away. Amazon is just about ruling the world because of the ability to have access to what we need when we need it. You need to be aware of how quickly your target market can access your business, not only for the products or services you provide, but also for the customer support. The access approach looks at how the customer first hears about your business to when they make their first purchase. I promise you that customers and clients care very much about how receptive you are to their feedback, and how available you are to support them.

Value, value, value. It is always about value and so very little about price. People pay for value. Time and time again, studies show that if people see value—even perceived value—they will normally pay whatever you are asking. You must be diligent in showcasing your business value. Your purple cow must be on full display at all times. Remember, your purple cow is your value proposition. It is why you are different than the rest. Your value sets your price.

Education brings it home with our S.A.V.E model. As an educator, I love this new approach. Provide your customers or clients with the most up-to-date information possible regarding your products or services. Make sure what you share with them is relevant. Have case studies and testimonials ready. Be able to show how your solution worked for others in the past. Case studies often show the benefits of using certain methods that are in alignment with your products or services. People are looking for proof. This is especially true in social entrepreneurship. You are going to be educating people on the truths of the wicked problems that you are addressing, and you are going to need to educate them on your solutions and how they will fit best in solving the problems and the IMPACT they will have in correcting the issues at hand.

With the space provided, I want you to spend a little time just brainstorming on the SAVE model and how it will work for your product or service. No pressure. Remember, you are just drafting. Allow your thoughts to come. Take a deep dive into your mind and give way to your brilliance as you develop thoughts regarding how you are going to use the SAVE model.

Let's now turn our attention to the marketing plan. For social entrepreneurs, we are not only selling a product or service, but we are selling the mission. We are already different because we are balancing purpose and profit. The way we start our marketing plan is by doing some research. Market research is a super important step. So how do you begin to do market research? Market research is the gathering and interpretation of data in a specific industry. It also includes answers to a series of questions, and, more importantly, the development of your target market.

There are two types of data that exist for market research: primary data and secondary data. Primary data is data you develop. You gather the information from doing research, test markets, surveys, focus groups, and so on. As a social entrepreneur, you will do a lot of primary research. There may not be too much secondary research available. Secondary data is data that already exists. The research has been done for you, and the information is published and available for use. As with any data, please be sure you check your sources. Make sure the sources are legitimate and reputable. Some of the information that you should be able to find out directly from secondary data is:

- *The total size of your industry*
- *Trends in the industry—is it growing or shrinking?*
- *The total size of your target market and what share is realistic for you to obtain*
- *Trends in the target market—is it growing or shrinking? How are customer needs or preferences changing?*

Below are a few additional questions that you should be able to answer from your research.

- *Who are your customers?*
- *What do they buy now?*
- *Why do they buy?*
- *When do they buy?*
- *What will make them buy from you?*

Who are your customers? This is one of the most important questions to answer. This is also known as your *target market*. I am always reminding my students and clients that they cannot serve everyone, nor do they really want to. Even though I do all I can to drill this into their heads, many times, they still come to me with a large target market. Then I remind them once again that they must bring in that market and be more focused. As social entrepreneurs, our market will be focused on the problem we are working to solve. If you are working on a solution for cancer, then you will target that market. But you will still need to choose segments. Your solution may not apply to all types of cancer. There are several different segments, but according to Active Marketing, an online branding and marketing research company, the list below contains the most common. Remember, you will not choose all of them. You will, however, select some.

- "**Psychographic:** *Grouping your customers into cultural clusters, social status, lifestyle, and personality type.*
- **Decision Makers:** *Grouping your customers based on who decides to purchase your product within the company structure.*
- **Behavioral:** *Grouping customers by product usage. For example, light, medium or heavy users. This stage also factors in brand loyalty and the type of user.*
- **Geographic:** *Grouping customers by a specific area, such regions of the country or state and urban or rural.*
- **Distribution:** *Grouping customers based on where they go to purchase your product, such as online, store or through a catalog.*
- **Demographic:** *Grouping customers by age, income level, gender, family size, religion, race, nationality, language, etc.*"[7]

I would like you to take a moment and start working on defining your target market. On the space provided, write out as much detail as you can regarding your target market. Remember to use the list provided above to help you develop. Your success or failure will be greatly reflected on how well you know the people you are serving. Remember, you are looking to make a lasting IMPACT, so you need to know who you have been called to serve. As I have stated, it will not be everyone. You will need to focus in, and the more do so, the more powerful your efforts will be. For this call-to-action activity, I want you to brainstorm—no pressure to get it right or wrong. Just make a list of who you think could be a protentional target, then circle your top three. Then I want you to decide on one to focus on to get started. Eventually, you will grow, but for now, I need you to get super focused and have a starting point.

The next part of the marketing plan is the marketing strategy, which starts with the company vision. The vision of the company addresses the question: Where is the company going? It addresses future goals or milestones yet to be accomplished. The mission of the company addresses the following questions:
1. Why does the business exist?
2. What do we do?
3. How do we do it?
4. For whom do we do it?

Both the vision and the mission provide direction for the company. For social entrepreneurs, this is our core. We are steering our ship with the use of both the mission and vision. We are selling our mission just as much, if not more than we are selling our product or service. In addition to creating your mission and your vision, you will also create values, goals, and objectives. Your values are tied in with your code of ethics, which you built earlier in the book. Values are one reason why someone would choose your product or service. Your values align with theirs. As social entrepreneurs, your values must be authentic, true in nature, deeply held in your own personal walk in life, and must be seen in your business transactions.

Goals and objectives will help you head for your destination. They are like a roadmap. You will start by setting goals. The dictionary defines a goal as *"the object of a person's ambition or effort; an aim or desired result."* Basically, a goal is what you want to achieve. Then we move on to setting objectives. Those are the steps we need to take in order to achieve the goals we have set in place. Next level steps required. For many years, marketing objectives have been known by an acronym called SMART: **S**pecific, **M**easurable, **A**chievable, **R**ealistic, and **T**ime-based. It is a new millennium, and we need to be SMARTER, so I have added two more objectives: **E**xecutable and **R**elevant.

At one point in my life, I weighed over 300 pounds. My vision was to be a normal body weight and, above all, healthy. That is where I was going. My mission was to embody health and a healthy lifestyle in pursuit of my vision. I tried to lose weight many times being SMART, but then I finally became SMARTER, and I want you to be a SMARTER social entrepreneur as well. I realized the objectives and critical steps I had to take to achieve my mission and, ultimately, the vision was every day. I needed to do a series of things that cultivated my new chosen lifestyle. I had to prep my food and eat the prepped food. I had to increase my water intake. I had to go to the gym. I had to do all of those steps consistently in order to achieve the results I desired. After a little over a year of discipline, staying focused on my vision, being true to my mission, and following the objectives I had laid out, I achieved one of my health goals of losing over 100 pounds. This is how the marketing strategy works. This is how many things in life work. Systems, strategy, and discipline.

I want you to take some time to think about your vision, mission, and objectives. This is your key message to those you serve and the world at large. I encourage you to do some research on other social enterprises to see how they have shaped their vision, mission, and values. You may find something you like, and, with just a little bit of wordplay, you could have a similar theme to theirs. Below, I listed some tips I believe are good to use when building a strong message. They are from Prosper Strategies, a social marketing enterprise company, and they are written by Alyssa Conrardy.

- "***Original:*** *Unique and specific to your social enterprise in order to differentiate it from others.*
- ***Short:*** *Longwinded and complicated messages are harder to remember. Keeping key messages short also makes them more adaptable.*
- ***Audience-centered:*** *Focused on the specific needs, interest and preference of your target market.*
- ***Linked to values/benefits:*** *Focused on the values you deliver and the benefits your social enterprise offers.*"[8]

Understand that your mission and vision don't need to be very long. They can be short and to the point. It really is up to you. As long as it resonates within you and you feel connected to it and it ties to your purpose, then I say go with it. You will reshape your vision and mission, but at the core, it will be and should be a solid foundation upon which you will build your social enterprise, one that is going to make an IMPACT and leave a lasting legacy. Don't hold back in drafting. No judgment on what you come up with. This is your time to draft, then you will select the best of the best. Just remember that a vision is for the long game, and the mission is the purpose for the people.

The marketing concept is also very important to understand. There are three components to the marketing concept: customer orientation, service orientation, and profit orientation. The customer orientation is all about finding out what the customers want and like, and then providing it to them. In entrepreneurship, the ability to find out what the customer wants has become increasingly easier. I can almost guarantee that you have some type of rewards card. Whether it is from a grocery store, drugstore, or you simply put your number into a system to collect points, we all have some type of rewards card. Well, these lovely rewards cards are tracking our every purchase. The data that is collected from the use of the reward card gives a company important information. It now knows what we like, how often we use products, and so on. The company will now send you coupons for a selected set of items they know you are going to buy. Brilliant!

Another way customer orientation is done is through conducting surveys. Surveys provide valuable information, as well. Companies use surveys all the time to not only provide customers with what they want but also to improve service. Service orientation is making sure everyone in the organization is committed to customer satisfaction. I started off this chapter by telling you that the greatest marketing tool you have is word of mouth—WOM. Service orientation is your key driver for WOM. You need everyone show-ready at all times. I am very customer service focused. It is truly a part of my purple cow, my value proposition. I stand out when it comes to customer satisfaction.

Due to my servant's mentality, I have been able to take little and make it much. I have been able to grow in locations, clients, and students, all because I know how important it is to provide excellent customer service. My clients and students, in turn, spread the word about me, and I grow again. Focusing on both customer orientation and service orientation is mission-critical to the success of your business, and the IMPACT you have been called to have.

Profit orientation focuses on the goods and services that will earn the most profit. This was the McDonalds' strategy when they first began. The McDonald brothers realized that what was selling and making the most profit were burgers, fries, and a drink. They eliminated everything else and focused just on that. It worked, and today, McDonald's is a billion-dollar business. This case is just one example, out of a million, of how to use a profit orientation. The key is to focus on what is selling and earning the most profit. That is the item or items you want to push. Keep that in mind as you look at your products or services. Do you really need all of them? Are they all making you money? Get rid of something and see how that works. You can always bring it back if you need to. Conversely, you cannot get back the lost time and money you spend on trying to sell something that no one wants to buy.

Marketing plans have many different elements to them. I have highlighted some of the most important in this chapter. In the back of the book, I have provided a standard template for you to refer to as you develop. There are other things you will need to do with your marketing plan, such as competitor analysis, developing a sales plan, and, of course, what budget you will set in order to accomplish your marketing needs. Most importantly, you will need to put the plan into action and then evaluate how the plan is working. After which you will make adjustments and keep what works, remove what doesn't, and hold some things for a later date in time. Making adjustments will take place time and time again in entrepreneurship, and in your life.

"Your brand is a gateway to your true work. You know you are here to do something—to create something or help others in some way. The question is, how can you set up your life and work so that you can do it? The answer lies in your brand. When you create a compelling brand, you attract people who want the promise of your brand—which you deliver."

—Dave Buck, leadership coach

Branding is defined by the business dictionary as *"the process involved in creating a unique name and image for a product in the consumers' mind, mainly through advertising campaigns with a consistent theme. Branding aims to establish a significant and differentiated presence in the market that attracts and retains loyal customers."*

I need you to understand that your brand is a promise to your customers, letting them know what they can expect from your offering and how it is different from others. Your logo is the face of your brand. It is part of how you will communicate your brand message and should be seen everywhere to grow brand awareness.

The business dictionary defines brand strategy as *"the long-term marketing support for a brand, based on the definition of the characteristics of the target consumers. It includes an understanding of their preferences, and expectations from the brand."* This brand message will be seen through ads, distribution, and packaging. Two of the most powerful and classic brands are Coca-Cola, which has managed to differentiate itself from other sodas through its consistent strategic branding, and Nike, which involves famous athletes as part of its branding strategy. Building a solid brand is going to start with a name. You may already have a name or thoughts of one, and then again, you may be struggling to come up with one. The next call-to-action activity will have you focus on name creation.

When you are creating your brand name, you need to be cautious of a few things. First, does someone else already have that name, and are they doing business under that name? You will need to find that out right away. Second, make sure your name can be understood. Have you ever seen the name of a business and thought, *Huh? How do you pronounce that? What does that mean?* You don't want a name that is too confusing, hard to spell, or hard to pronounce. It should not have any underlying message that only you know. It needs to be fresh and timeless because you will want it to be with you the entire time you are in business. There is power in a name, so choose wisely.

You might be asking yourself, *"How do I even come up with a name in the first place?"* I would encourage you to go to a quiet place, a place that works with your highest element—water, fire, air, or earth. Sit in that quiet place and allow whatever to come to you regarding your business and name. Write down everything that comes. Just as in all the other activities, you are brainstorming. No judgment. Just allow your thoughts to come. Don't throw anything away at first. Then go back through your list and examine what you have. Just don't be too harsh on yourself. After you come up with a few name choices, you can then take it to your friends, family, and even your potential target market and ask them what they think about your name selections. Let them tell you and be open to receive the feedback. This is what I did with the book title for my first book, *Entrepreneurship Empowered*. The original title I had was 21st Century Entrepreneurship, but it fell flat. I then came up with a few other selections of titles and subtitles that I sent out to my target market, and, boom! *Entrepreneurship Empowered* rose to the top and was a much better fit than 21st Century Entrepreneurship. I have provided space for you to work on your name. Remember, just let everything possible to come to you, without self-censoring.

There are steps to building your brand. You will certainly need a logo. Many times, the logo is all we see. Take, for example, Starbucks—if you look at most of their products, their name is not on them, just their logo. The same is true with their storefront and store signs. Their logo has gained enough awareness that we know the little funny-looking mermaid lady in a circle is Starbucks. We don't quite know why that is their logo and what it has to do with coffee, but we recognize it, nonetheless. It is unique, and it has been undoubtedly instrumental in the success of the brand. Your logo could start off with your name on it, as Starbucks' did, but any good logo will eventually hold ground with no name needed. That is called brand awareness. The evolution of the Starbucks logo went from having the name on the logo, as well as the language coffee, tea, and spices, and then it changed to just coffee. Then, finally, nothing. No name, no product. Just that funny-looking mermaid.

To go along with your logo, you will want to create a tagline, also known as a slogan. One of the more well-known taglines is Nike's *"Just Do It."* This tagline has been around since the late 1980s. Talk about power in a slogan! Let's now have a little fun. Below are some well-known taglines. Take a moment to read them over and see if you can figure out the companies they belong to.

Kid Tested. Mother Approved.
Life's Good
Trusted Everywhere
Maybe She's Born With It
We Try Harder
Keep Walking
Gather 'Round the Good Stuff
Makes Mouths Happy
Something Special in the Air
It's Not Just a Job, It's an Adventure!

How do you think you did? The answers are in the back of the book. Don't cheat and look now if you didn't try. If you did try, look now to see how you did. You might surprise yourself. I'm sure you did well with the taglines given. That is how the programming of marketing works. The essence of your brand message is found in the tagline, and that is why it must be short, simple, clear, and, most of all, memorable. It may be difficult to do, but I am sure you can do it. For my business STFF, my tagline is *"The Better Solution."* I can promise you that I am always looking for better solutions. Not only do I look for them, but I provide them. My tagline is living, and yours should be as well.

Once you develop your logo and your tagline, you need to put those suckers on everything possible. I mentioned earlier in the chapter that your clients and customers need to have some swag. Swag helps build your brand. Swag is everything from T-shirts to coffee cups to notepads, and the list goes on. Of course, it will go on your packaging labels, letterheads, business cards, flyers, pens, and so forth. Then make sure all your clients receive something from you with your logo on it. My STFF logo was on everything, from the fax order form to the packaging label to the bright yellow invoice. I even had T-shirts made that my staff and I wore and that I would give to my clients when I came around and visited them. I am big on branding. Part of your brand is also your appearance. Today, I am known for my shoes: high heels. It is part of my brand. I am also known for snapping my fingers. I am the "Snap Queen." That, too, is a part of my brand.

There are many things that contribute to your brand and the awareness your brand attracts. Make sure you take the time to develop your brand and remember to always deliver on your brand promise. Rules were meant to be broken, but promises were not. Keep your word and keep your promise. This is extremely important for social entrepreneurs because we are seen in a different light. We are not in the game for only profit but rather purpose, and those who hold great purpose learn how important it is to keep their word.

As I close this chapter, I am leaving you with one of my favorite call-to-action activities. One that I believe you will truly enjoy. You are the brand. Below is a self-assignment. I make all my students, regardless of what class they are in, do this assignment. I also have my clients work through the same assignment. It is so powerful that I need everyone to have it. I promise it will be a lot of fun. I want you to ask five to seven people to describe you in three words. Tell them that you will not be upset by what they say if they do need to say something that could be a little hard to swallow. You need to know. Tell them not to think very long but say whatever three words come to mind. Make sure you write them down. If you see a word pop up more than once, make sure to circle that word. It may happen with a few words. Then you are going to reflect on what you have been told. The words that popped up a few times are your strongest brand traits. Now, do you agree or disagree with the way you were described? Write about it.

How people see you is your brand. You need to be aware of how you are being seen. The next part of this assignment is to create a mantra or tagline. A mantra is short and to the point. This mantra is for your life. Not for a business, but for you. The next step is to create a logo. Design yourself a personal logo. I am going to provide you with my examples of how I did this assignment, and then there will be space provided for you to write your answers. You may also want to use a computer to do this work.

Self-Branding Assignment example:

- Words that describe me:
    - Creative, Bold, Giving
    - Giving, Passionate, Leader
    - Bold, Driven, Gritty
    - Aggressive, Brave, Creative
    - Strong, Giving, Leader
    - Passionate, Bold, Driven

- o Resilient, Gritty, Giving
  - ➢ I would have to agree with the words that others have used to describe me. I know some of my core strengths are being a leader, creative, and I love to give. I can be aggressive from time to time, but I would hope others would not be too taken aback by my aggressive traits.
- Mantra/Tagline:
  - o Empowered Encourager
  - o Logo:

N M P

Hopefully you enjoyed that activity, as well as the other ones in this chapter. They will do you well as you build your social enterprise, and even more so, your legacy. I want you to remember you are a builder, and you have a great purpose. You are going to make an IMPACT as long as you don't give up the fight to do so. I am always working to master my masteries. Mastering your mind is number one in the pursuit of mastery. We discussed that earlier in the book. Mastering your message is going to be the next important step you take, and it will lead you to mastering your market. Both the creation of the message and understanding the market have been touched on in this chapter, but I encourage you to do additional research. You will need to do so in order to become a master of marketing.

American author Robert Greene's fifth book is titled *Mastery*. It is a book that explores the lives of some of the greats, such as Darwin, Mozart, and Ford. There is a very powerful quote in the book that I am now going to leave you with, and then I will give you one more final mastery to pursue. "*What you are trying to create will not magically take off after a few creative bursts of inspiration but must be slowly evolved through a step-by-step process as you correct the flaws. In the end, you win through superior craftsmanship, not marketing. The craftsmanship involves creating something with an elegant, simple structure, getting the most out of your materials—a high form of creativity.*" I would like for you to read that one more time. Then let it breathe within you. You are not creating a brand that is just here and gone. You are creating one that is going to live beyond you. This is what I need for you to understand and fully grasp. It will take time to build such an empire, but it can be done. You will use all the elements that I have shared so far and many others. It will not happen overnight. I need you to always be in pursuit of mastery. As we turn the page into the next chapter, the final "M" I need you to master is your money. If you don't master your money, I can promise it will master you.

Chapter 6

Funding Your Social Venture

"If we command our wealth, we shall be rich and free. If our wealth commands us, we are poor indeed."

—Edmund Burke, philosopher

How well do you handle your money? You will need to master your money, or, just as I stated at the end of Chapter Five, it will master you. The above quote is true in that we will stay poor if we are commanded by our money. We have the power to command money and grow our wealth. Did you know the wealthy have a language all their own? Well, they do. They understand the true meaning of assets and liabilities. They speak stocks, bonds, mutual funds, and securities. They pay attention to the flow of money not only in our country, but the world. They also understand another valuable Palumbo Principle: Pay yourself first. This principle is a key to financial freedom. It requires self-discipline. It is not easy to pay yourself first, especially when the bills are due, the rent needs to be paid, you need food to eat, and so on. Of course, you want to make sure you take care of your needs to live—please don't get me wrong—but far too often, people don't have a money problem, they have a spending problem. People are wasteful with their money. It commands them and they stay poor. It is not your salary that makes you rich, but rather your spending habits.

I make all my students track their money. This is one of the best ways to figure out what is really going on with your finances. The longer you can track, the better. I have my students track for two weeks. However, I would say that if you can track for a month up to three months, you will have some good data. You must track it to the penny. Always keep a little book with you and don't miss one cent. Seriously, to the penny. Once you have tracked your money, you will then need to reflect and have a come-to-Jesus moment with yourself. Now, if you are already savvy and smart with your money, that is great; I would still ask you to see how you could level up and become even wiser. What little pleasures are you indulging in that could be cut so that you could further invest in yourself or your business?

You need to become emotionally intelligent when it comes to your money. One component of emotional intelligence is having the ability to say "no" to people, places, and things. Say no to eating out so much. Say no to buying coffee every day. Say no to giving others your money when you need it for yourself. There are many things you need to say no to, and I need you to understand you have the right to say NO! If you wish to be matrix-free, you will need to stop feeding the matrix. Knowing how to manage your money is a must. If you don't know how to manage your money, then you surely will not know how to manage a business's money. Poor financial planning and mismanaging of funds are two of the main reasons why businesses fail. As social entrepreneurs, the money part of the business, in my opinion, is one of the hardest parts. So, track your money and remember to pay yourself first. Truly open your mind and make the shift of being controlled by money to mastering it.

"An abundance mentality springs from internal security, not from external rankings, comparisons, opinions, possessions, or associations."

—Stephen Covey, educator and author

Mindset is everything. Our minds are extremely powerful. It has taken me years upon years to rewire my brain. With regard to money, I am still learning, just like each of you. I am certainly wiser today than I was in the past. There is a survival mindset, and there is an abundant mindset. The survival mindset will have you forever stuck in poverty. I lived in a survival mindset for a very long time. Even when I was sitting on six figures and money was flowing everywhere, I still lived in a survival mindset due to my tragic backstory. The programing is real, my friends. This is why I encourage you to do the work needed to rewire your brain and break free from the matrix. For me, it has taken intense work. As I began to heal myself and awaken, I realized how powerful my mind was and how much I had the ability to create what I desired to see. I experienced a mind shift. I deliberately worked on my thinking, and even more so, on how I spoke. There is power in our words and in our thoughts. We do truly live in an abundant world, but it is up to us to see as such and to speak it into our daily lives. I give much gratitude for my abundance. I know that I will never be poor again. I have internal security.

Let us now turn our attention to some basic accounting. If you haven't taken an accounting class, I highly encourage you to take one. When I purchased STFF, Dan encouraged me to take a managerial accounting class just to give me a foundation for understanding accounting and financial planning. I now give that same recommendation to all my students and clients. I often remind my students that it is perfectly fine to hire someone smarter than you. However, don't you ever not **know your numbers**. If you don't know your accounting, someone could take advantage of you. I have seen it happen. Don't let that happen to you. Take the class, know your numbers, pay attention, and be aware of what is going on with your business numbers.

There are a few financial reports I want you to become familiar with: The *income statement*, *balance sheet*, and *cash flow*. In the back of the book, I have given charts for you to see what each one of them looks like. The **income statement** is a financial report that measures the financial performance of your business on a monthly or annual basis.

The income statement tells you just that: how much income (profit/loss) you made. As I stated in the previous paragraph, it is also called the profit and loss statement, because it will show both. I want you to always be in the black. Not the red. If you haven't heard the saying *being in the black or red*, let me tell you what it means. The **black means profit**, and the **red means loss.** Some businesses do go into the red. It is common for start-ups to be in the red, but you don't want to stay there. You simply cannot stay there and survive in business.

The **balance sheet** is a financial report that shows what the company owes and what it owns, including shareholders' stake, at a particular point in time. The balance sheet has a particular formula, which, again, must be balanced. This is the fundamental accounting equation: Assets = Liabilities + Owner's Equity. The balance sheet is going to show you the big picture, help you measure the value of your business, and can serve as an early warning sign. The balance sheet is also something that current or potential investors will want to look at and interpret. They will want to know how their investment is doing or will do.

I am sure by this point you are wondering, *What do all these different accounting terms mean?* After I introduce you to the third and final report, *cash flow*, I will be providing you with some key accounting terms. I need you to become familiar with the meanings of those terms. You can find a list of accounting terms and definitions in the back of the book for your reference, as well. The **cash flow statement** is a financial report that details the inflows and outflows of cash for a company over a set period of time. You always want to be aware of your flow of cash. *Cash is king*. I know you have heard that before, right? If not, well, now you have. Understanding the flow of cash is critical in business. It will show you if you have enough cash on hand to pay for your current liabilities. Here is where money management really comes into play. You must know how to handle the money in the most effective and efficient way. You must be wise with your business spending habits, just as you need to be wise with your personal spending habits. The cash flow statement has three components, though not all businesses use all three:

1. *Cash from operating activities*
2. *Cash from investing activities*
3. *Cash from financing activities*

The operating activities is the most commonly used component in small business. It will consider the current expenses, as well as the current accounts receivable. The cash flow statement complements the balance sheet and income statement and is a mandatory part of a company's financial reports since 1987. It's still required today in entrepreneurship.

We are now going to turn our attention to the break-even analysis (aka break-even point). One of the very first things Dan taught me about the business was the break-even point. Remember me stating earlier how he recommended I take a managerial class? Well, in that same conversation, he introduced me to the break-even point. He actually worked the break-even point for STFF with me in his home office in Berkeley. The business dictionary defines the break-even analysis as the *"study of the mathematical relationship between costs and sales revenue, under a given set of assumptions regarding the firm's fixed costs and variable costs. In this financial analysis, the objective is to determine (in manufacturing) the number of products that must be sold at a given price to cover the costs, or (in project financing) number of months or years required by the forecasted total net cash flow to equal estimated total project cost. An integral part of financial planning, it is performed either by using a breakeven-formula or by drawing a breakeven graph."* You must understand your break-even point. It is very important, along with the other reports you have now been introduced to. In the back of the book, I've provided some accounting terms and definitions. Make sure you take time to review them.

"The revenue engine is a whole system. It encompasses a diverse set of integrated components, each doing its part to advance the system's purpose. The engine is not just comprised of marketing and sales—it includes product, accounting, and the underlying technology and data infrastructure required to keep everything flowing. It involves people, tools, workflow, and metrics. Its purpose is to optimize reach, conversion, and expansion of customer spend."

—Tom Mohr, serial entrepreneur and Fortune 500 executive

Now that you have a little more information regarding accounting, I want to dive deeper into the revenue model. A revenue model *"describes the structure of how a company generates revenue or income. Each customer segment can contain one or more revenue streams."* As a social entrepreneur, you must understand the revenue model, and you must have a revenue strategy. You are going to start by asking yourself what your revenue streams are and what is your pricing. Your streams will be the strategy, and the price will be the tactics used. Revenues streams have three questions to answer:
1. What value are customers willing to pay?
2. How do customers pay today?
3. How much are they currently paying?

There are many different revenue strategies. I am going to share a few with you, but I also encourage you to do additional research on this topic, as you may find in your research a better solution for your social enterprise.

Unit sales measures the amount of revenue generated by the number of items (units) sold by a company. This is the one I used in my business. My revenue was generated by the number of files I sold. The more files I sold, the more money I made. The **subscription model** is an ever-growing strategy, and to be honest with you, it is absolutely brilliant. A subscription revenue model charges a customer for continual use of the product and or service. Do you have Netflix? Or better yet, Amazon Prime? Those are both subscription strategies. The **freemium revenue** model is one of my favorites. Who doesn't love something free? According to an article in the *Harvard Business Review* titled, "Making 'Freemium' Work, by Vineet Kumar, *"'freemium'—a combination of 'free' and 'premium'—has become the dominant business model among internet start-ups and smartphone app developers. Users get basic features at no cost and can access richer functionality for a subscription fee."*[9] The freemium model offers a product or service for free, but then you pay a premium for advanced features. Dropbox is a great example of this strategy. You get free storage up to 2GB, but then if you pay $9.99 per month for the pro plan, you can get up to 1 TB, which is significantly more space.

Fee for service model is another strategy I use. As a consultant and coach, I charge a fee for my services. I have different packages that I offer for my services, and my clients pay me by the hour. You may also want to consider using a **licensing model**. A licensing model is defined as *"a business arrangement in which one company gives another company permission to manufacture its product for a specified payment."*

As a social entrepreneur, you may invent something that you will sell only the licenses to use. You will retain ownership but allow other companies the right to use your products. We have already touched on intellectual property (IP). If you are looking at the licensing model, you will want to ensure you take all the proper steps with your IP and seek legal advice.

To close out the models, I am going to now turn to the **donation model**. This is one that you will use in the nonprofit world. This is not to say for-profits don't receive donations, because they do. I don't know a nonprofit that doesn't accept donations. For the work I do with the STEEL Legacy, I rely heavily on donations. Wikipedia is a company that depends on donations, as they give their services away for free. If you plan to go into the nonprofit side of the house, you will need to do all the research you can on how the donation model works and all the work it takes to ensure you do receive all you need. I am the backbone to STEEL Legacy, so no matter what donations I receive or don't receive, I will go and get whatever is needed. I fully support and fund my outreaches in order to serve the homeless. I need you to fully understand this part of the business because the same is true in entrepreneurship. You will need to make sure you are able to invest in your own business.

"Price is what you pay. Value is what you get."

—Warren Buffett, CEO of Berkshire Hathaway

We just covered a few different revenue streams, and now we are going to turn our attention to pricing. This is the second part of the revenue model. Remember, people pay for value. The more you know how much people value your products or services, the better you can set your price. There are two types of pricing models: **fixed and dynamic**. Fixed is just that. It is a price that is set, and a customer will either pay the price or pass on buying. The dynamic model is not fixed, and the price is different for each customer. There are two ways to break down dynamic pricing: segmented pricing and negotiated pricing. I am sure when you read negotiated pricing, you think of car sales. That is exactly right. It is where you go back and forth until both the buyer and the seller believe they have reached a fair price. Segmented pricing, on the other hand, sells a product or service at a different price, not because of the cost to create, but rather because of the different geographical location or by the perception of the consumer.

What are some ways to set your pricing using the fixed price model? You get to decide. One of the most common ways is to do cost plus markup. You take what it costs you to make the product, and then you mark it up. For example, if it costs you $50.00 to make your product, then a general rule of thumb is to markup 100%. You will then sell your product for $100.00. Now, if your customer holds a greater value in your product, you could set the price based on value. They may find the value in the product to be $150.00 or even $200.00, and therefore, you set your price accordingly. Another way to set your fixed price is by volume. When you set the price in volume, it is based on the number of products you buy. The more a client or customer buys, the lower the price for the product. I use this same model with my consulting and coaching. The more you buy, the lower the price for my service.

You will need to try different ways of setting your price, and you will also need to try different strategies to see which one works the best for you, your business, and even your industry. Regardless of which way you go, you will always need to ensure you are covering your cost to produce your products or service. If you are providing a service like coaching and consulting, you will need to set a price floor, meaning you cannot go any lower than a set amount or it is simply not worth your time. You need to remember to never undervalue your time and yourself. When you have a product, there will be cost in not only producing the product but running the business. This is why I gave the break-even analysis earlier in the chapter. You will need to understand what all your fixed costs are and what all your variable costs are.

Let's break down some of the start-up costs you will likely incur as a new business. Keep in mind there is no cookie-cutter recipe for businesses. Each business is going to have different needs and expenses. There is no one-size-fits-all financial solution. You are going to need to make a start-up expenses worksheet. There are several different templates available that you can download and type directly into. The following are common start-up costs you are likely to have, regardless of what business type:

- Office space
- Equipment and supplies
- Communications
- Utilities
- Licenses and permits
- Insurance
- Inventory
- Employee salaries
- Advertising, marketing, and market research
- Printed marketing material
- Making a website
- Lawyers and accountants

Don't underestimate your start-up cost. Do your research. I would even encourage you to add 5–10% to each of your start-up costs. I would rather you have excess than be short. When doing your research for start-up costs, it is wise to reach out to someone who is in a similar field of business and ask them what costs they have incurred. Normally, others in business are open to speaking with aspiring entrepreneurs. If someone says no, then just keep searching until you find someone.

Once you know your start-up costs and how much money you will need to fund your business, you can start looking for investors or small business loans. For me, I was self-funded. I had enough money generating that I didn't need to take any loans out for STFF. I used the money I generated to scale STFF some business; however, I will take out small business loans and use it for growing. I will go into loans in just a bit. For many of you, self-funding is all you will have. You must be able to fund your own business ventures and have some stake in the game regardless. Why? Because someone is not going to come along and just invest in you without you having some investment in the business yourself.

Crowdfunding is a new way of funding. I'm sure many of you have already been exposed to some form of crowdfunding. Crowdfunding is used in many ways, not just in business, but it seems to be most successful in business. The word tells you about its meaning: a crowd of people come together to fund your business. Crowdfunding is not a loan. The money you receive doesn't need to be paid back. In some cases, it is like a prepayment for your product or service. In others, it is more an offering of support in exchange for some swag, which could be a T-shirt, a coffee cup, or the like. The Crowdfunding Center's May 2014 report identified two primary types of crowdfunding:

1. *Rewards crowdfunding: entrepreneurs pre-sell a product or service to launch a business concept without incurring debt or sacrificing equity/shares.*
2. *Equity crowdfunding: the backer receives shares of a company, usually in its early stages, in exchange for the money pledged.*

The SBA has some awesome tutorials regarding crowdfunding. I highly recommend you take a look at them. With crowdfunding, you must be fully committed to the process. You must understand that even though it is a fantastic opportunity for a small business to enter, not all small businesses should do so. It certainly should not be taken lightly. You will need to make sure you don't miss one call or email. You will need to make sure you are pitching your business on a daily basis. You will need to make sure you are focused on your target market. You must plan how you are going to create a buzz and keep it going. You are also going to need to have a solid plan. It doesn't need to be some in-depth formal business plan, but it does need to have some key drivers. These include market research, competitive analysis, financials, and expected return.

There are many different crowdfunding sites in the market today. I would like for you to do a little research on the following top four. Make notes as you research, using the space provided. You should be able to find pros and cons, as well as important information, such as how much of a cut they take from what you raise, and whether there are any additional charges. The research you gather will help you to select which site is best for your business needs. The top four sites are *Kickstarter, GoFundMe, Indiegogo, and Patreon.*

Loans are a lump sum of money you receive, commonly from a bank or other financial institution. You pay back loans with interest. The SBA backs 80% of small business loans in the United States. They don't lend you the money, remember, they only back you. You must be credit-worthy for any loan. Your business must be in good financial standing and have a solid foundation. Typically for a business loan, you need a traditional business plan that must include an expense sheet and financial projections for up to five years. We covered business plans earlier in the book, and in the back of the book is the standard business plan template that the SBA uses. If you recall, I advised you to pay for someone to write your plan for you. I am once again making that same recommendation—if you are seeking a loan and a large one at that, please pay for a professional to help you write the plan. You will be more likely to receive the funding you need. Now, if your credit is not right and your business is not in good financial standing, then please don't waste your time. You will not get a loan. It is as simple as that.

Finding an investor is another way to receive funding for your business. There are two types of **investors**: angel investors and venture capitalists. They are both very different. An angel investor is normally a very wealthy person who provides funding to a business startup in exchange for convertible debt or ownership equity. Angel investors are often retired entrepreneurs or executives who may be interested in angel investing for reasons that go beyond pure monetary return. These include wanting to keep abreast of current developments in a particular business arena, mentoring another generation of entrepreneurs, and making use of their experience and networks on a less-than-full-time basis. Thus, in addition to funds, angel investors can often provide valuable management advice and important contacts.

Venture capitalists, on the other hand, provide funding after an initial seed funding has already been given. Seed funding could come from crowdfunding or an angel investor.

Venture capitalists commonly take on high-risk companies for a high return. A venture capitalist is a person who makes venture investments, and these venture capitalists are expected to bring managerial and technical expertise as well as capital to their investments. A venture capital fund refers to a pooled investment vehicle (in the United States, often an LP or LLC) that primarily invests the financial capital of third-party investors in enterprises that are too risky for the standard capital markets or bank loans. These funds are typically managed by a venture capital firm, which often employs individuals with technology backgrounds, business training, and/or deep industry experience.

As a social entrepreneur, all the different funding sources given will work; however, there are a few more ways that that are specific to the work of social enterprises. It is time once again to put your researcher hat on. I am going to provide you with six different programs that I want you to research. Each of the following organizations funds social endeavors. They may even decide to fund yours.

- Acumen Fund
- Echoing Green
- Ashoka
- Verb U (Dell Social Innovation)
- Y Combinator
- Fast Forward

Nonprofits have a bit of a harder time with regard to funding. The bulk of their funding will come from donations and grants. I am a grant writer. I didn't really realize I was until I had a college professor tell me that I was. He insisted that I do a research paper on grant writing and explore grants at all angles. I have written and won both public and private grants. Grant writing is a great skill to have, and I encourage those of you who are writers to really explore and research how to write grants. There are not just nonprofit grants, but there are also for-profit business grants. However, as I wrap up this chapter, I am going to focus on the nonprofit side of the house. I encourage those of you who are going to take the nonprofit road to find your local nonprofit resource center. If you reside in the Sacramento area, there is a resource center called the Impact Foundry. They are open to the public and offer classes and tons of resources for nonprofits. There are many nonprofit resources across the U.S. Make sure that, again, if that is the road you are going to take, you find a center near you and visit it.

There are federal, state, and city grants available. Grant applications are long and cumbersome, but they are worth it. You will certainly need a turtle to help you with all the details that are involved. Grants do have certain criteria that must be met, so not every grant will work for you and your organization. You can do a grant search using the internet. There's normally always contact information, and it is perfectly fine to reach out to whoever is listed and ask questions or receive clarification. Grants do have a window of time that you must submit either your quote or proposal. Request for Quote or Request for Proposal is how many grants will be listed. RFQ and RFP for short.

Another way to fund a nonprofit is by sponsorships. According to an article written by Allison Gauss titled, "There's More Than One Way to Fund a Nonprofit," "*sponsorships allow nonprofits to partner with other reputable organizations to receive funds and in-kind donations. Companies and organizations may sponsor a nonprofit as a general partnership or in conjunction with a campaign or event. The sponsor, though, will expect some sort of recognition or promotion of their brand too. Usually, this comes in the form of public thanks and displaying the sponsor's logo. This is especially apparent at events like charity run/walks."*[10]

Events are another way to raise funds for an organization. I had the honor of volunteering for a women's center locally in Sacramento. Wellspring Women's Center is a wonderful place started by two nuns. The center feeds women and children Monday through Friday. They also provide an array of workshops, social services, and events. I was a photographer for them and often came in on Thursdays to help with their art corner. One of their biggest fundraisers was a dinner and silent auction. They would raise a considerable amount of money from this one event, and it all went to good use. When you are choosing to do an event, you must always keep in mind the expenses. They can eat into the money raised if not taken into account. I also want you to think creatively when it comes to an event. I think one of the best fundraising events I was able to attend was one where purses were in the center of the table as centerpieces. They were available for purchase, and that was one part of the event. There was also a silent auction.

What exactly is a silent auction? According to Bidding Owl, an online auction solution management service, *"During a silent auction, bids are written on a sheet of paper that is commonly placed before or next to the item. At the predetermined end of the auction, the highest listed bidder wins the item. This auction is often used in charity events, with many items auctioned simultaneously and 'closed' at a common finish time. The auction is 'silent' in that no auctioneer is selling individual items. At charity auctions, bid sheets usually have a fixed starting amount, predetermined bid increments, and a 'guaranteed bid' an amount which works the same as a 'buy now' amount. Many non-profits have turned to silent auctions either as stand-alone events or as a way to maximize the revenue from an ongoing fundraising event."*[11]

Donations are one of the top ways nonprofits receive their funding, and they are the largest part of the funding funnel. I personally cannot do what I do without donations and volunteers. The following information comes from the same article referenced above by Allison Gauss:

"*Online Giving* – It has never been easier to give to a nonprofit organization. In the past, you would have to physically hand over your donation or send it through the mail. Now, anyone can simply enter their billing information and click the 'Donate' button to support a cause.

Monthly Giving – One advantage of the move to online giving has been the facilitation of painless recurring giving programs. Monthly giving is a smart way to create a sustainable stream of revenue at your nonprofit. Having reliable monthly income allows organizations to plan for the future and break out of the financial mindset of feast and famine. Monthly donors also have higher retention rates than the general giving community and ultimately give more in their donor lifetime.

Peer-to-Peer Fundraising – With peer-to-peer you can grow your community and empower existing supporters to go above and beyond a modest donation. P2P fundraising allows supporters to create fundraising pages and reach out and appeal to their friends and family to give. Rather than making a single gift, which is limited to an individual's financial means, the fundraiser leverages their social network to raise both funds and awareness. Every gift to a supporter's fundraising page provides you with a new contact.

Major Donors – Major donors are a special category of individual donors. These are supporters with the financial means to give more than most. Each nonprofit defines major gifts differently. For a small nonprofit, $250 might be a major gift, while a larger organization may define it as gifts of $5,000 or more. Whatever your nonprofit's threshold for major gifts, this type of support requires ongoing cultivation and communication. The process of courting and retaining major donors is often called 'Moves Management.'"[10]

We have covered much in this chapter. I highly recommend that you not only go back through and read it over again, but I encourage you to do additional research. I can't provide you with everything you need in regard to funding and financial planning. I only gave you enough to get started. If you attend one of my classes at the college, you will go even deeper with me, as you will be developing a financial plan for social enterprises. It is by doing the work that we learn the work. Make sure you don't sit on your research and all the knowledge you've gained. I need you to take it and run with it. No pressure to get anything right. You may just fail, and that is perfectly fine. What you will not do is stay in failure. You will get up, dust yourself off, and keep it moving. Learn from what you did, make adjustments, and go at it again. Take the time you need to gather all the information that is relevant for your social enterprise and then give it a try. Remember, I need you to know your numbers. Pay yourself first. Don't you dare let your money master you. You are the master of your money.

Chapter 7
Leadership, Human Capital, and Volunteers

"Train people well enough so they can leave. Treat them well enough so they don't have to."

—Sir Richard Branson, serial entrepreneur

You are in the human economy. It has always been here. You see, no matter which economy we have been in, from agriculture to technology, it has taken the human to produce the work. Yes, even with technology. We need the human to create the technology, and then, when it breaks down, we need the human to come and fix it. Technology will never overtake the human economy because the human has a set of skills that technology will never have. We are unique. We have a soul and emotions. That is something technology will never have. At least I hope not. That is where things could really go wrong. It is the emotions that cause us to do many of the things we do. This is why emotional intelligence in leadership is absolutely necessary.

I want you for a moment to think about some great leaders. They can be anyone from celebrities to bosses to family, even fictional characters. Think about what it was that made them such great leaders. If they are personal leaders to you, what do you really admire about them? Why did you see them as such great leaders? Then I want you to think about what types of behaviors they had. What type of spirit did they carry? Then, for a moment, I want you to think about the concept of being a born leader versus being able to build a leader. In the space provided, write what comes to your mind about all I have asked.

Are leaders made, or are they born? I swear I came out of the womb saying, *"Charge, forward we go!"* For the longest time, I really felt like I was a natural born leader, and that all great leaders must have been born that way. Many of you may feel the same way, too. However, I will tell you that leaders can be made. I am in the business of building up people, and I believe that a true leader is one who will build up more leaders, not followers. I also believe it is extremely important to take care of your people—those who work for you, as well as those you serve.

"The supreme quality for leadership is unquestionably integrity. Without it, no real success is possible..."

—Dwight D. Eisenhower, U.S. president

Leaders commonly have a core set of qualities. Though each leader is different in their own right, there does tend to be a theme with many of the greatest leaders of all time. *Honesty and integrity* are often right at the top of the list of qualities. As social entrepreneurs, you already know how important it is to be honest and have integrity. Truly, it would be very hard for us to be any other way. This is where we can differ from other businesses and leaders. There are many leaders out there in the business world that are not honest, nor do they have integrity. They are driven by greed, which creates a poor work culture. You can look at the Enron case and see that corrupt leadership only leads to corrupt business. If you haven't heard about or don't know about the Enron case, I recommend you examine it. The Enron case will hold space for a very long time as an example of what not to do in business. It is one of the most highly discussed and studied ethics cases in the U.S. and around the world.

Confidence is critical to leadership. Especially because leadership is about inspiring others. Please don't confuse arrogance with confidence. Arrogant leaders are often single-minded. They believe they are superior. They may be highly intelligent but socially inept. You know someone like that, don't you? Confident leaders don't need to offend others. They see the potential in others and have a desire to help them succeed. Confident leaders will rarely tell you how wrong you are. They will certainly give you advice on how to be a better person. They will never put you down for being human. Arrogant leaders, however, will ridicule you and often belittle you, even in front of your peers. So much bullying goes on in the workplace, and, as a result, the employee turnover rate is extremely high. So is poor performance.

Being an effective communicator is mandatory in being an effective leader. Effective communication not only comes from speaking, but also listening and observation. All great leaders will take time out to listen to those under their command. They will also observe, in order to hear what isn't spoken. Then they will take all of what they have learned and received and use it when they communicate their message. This is where emotional intelligence will come into play. Observing the body language of a person, the tone in which they are speaking, how their energy is, and if they are in a state of elevated emotion are all key in being able to communicate successfully and understand what is going on.

Words are powerful. I am big on speaking life not only over myself and my children, but to everyone I encounter. Again, I am in the business of building up people. I must speak life. There is so much power in our words. *"I am..."* is by far the most powerful statement of all, because what you put after, you will ultimately be. Two other little words that are very powerful too is, THANK YOU! I cannot tell you how often those two little words are so underused yet have so much power to them. You, I am sure, have done many things in your life and have not received a thank you. Well, guess what? Right now, I say THANK YOU! As social entrepreneurs, we should be much kinder, and "thank you" should be a part of our daily lives. It is super important to make sure to not only speak life over your people, but also to thank them for doing a great job. You have no business without them.

Humility is a key core competency of a leader. I have more power on the ground in a place of humility than I do standing above you, screaming and waving my hands around like a crazy lady—which I can do, mind you, because I am an Italian who gets loud and talks with her hands. Being humble and using emotional intelligence allows me to hold space for others, make sound decisions, and even be more creative. All of which are very important to leadership. A study to look at is that of Ou, Waldman, and Peterson published in the *Journal of Management* in 2015 entitled "Do Humble CEOs Matter?" This study of 105 IT companies found that greater humility in their CEOs was associated with greater leadership team integration, greater collaboration and cooperation, and greater flexibility in strategic orientation.[12]

Humble leaders are working toward the good of others and society, not themselves. Humble leaders stay hungry. They never stop learning, they are authentic in every way, they give up being right, and they give way to asking the right questions. They have a servant's heart and understand the true power of service. We, as social entrepreneurs who are going to make a lasting IMPACT in this world, will hold humility at our core and never let go. It is part of our brilliance.

Brilliance takes many forms—emotional intelligence is certainly one form. It allows you to have acute awareness with regard to your own emotions and those whom you serve. That acute awareness is crucial for sound decision making, which we all know is required in leadership. With regard to others, you can create strategies that keep them grounded as you deliver either good or bad news. Mental health is an epidemic in our world. The jungle is filled with the craziest animals you have ever seen. You are one of them. (Don't look at my words like that, you know I am telling the truth. You get hangry, too!).

Emotionally intelligent leaders tend to have a better grasp on mental health and are able to assess the mental state of their employees. They know if someone is suffering from depression, anxiety, grief, trauma, and the like. They are then able to serve them by providing the resources they need. Being supportive has a direct effect on the productivity of the business. The healthier the employees, the healthier the company. As social entrepreneurs, we are fighting the wicked problems, and it will be very taxing on not only yourself, but also those you work with. This is not easy work. Your team may be affected by what they see and learn. I know from working with disability law that it is very hard to read about all the hurt and sickness people are suffering from. You will need to keep in mind that your people will need emotional breaks; let's call it a mental health day. Yes, they are with you to fight the good fight, and it will make them feel great by doing meaningful work, but they are still humans and ones who care deeply. They will need balance, and as their leader, you are going to need to make sure that is in place.

"Leadership is an action, not a position."

—Donald McGannon, broadcasting executive

Leaders take action and remain calm under pressure. If a building is on fire, you are going to find the true leader getting everyone out of the building. They are not in a state of panic. I remember it like it was yesterday. Dan Acland, the man I worked for and bought my business from, told me something I have never forgotten: *"When the plane is crashing, DO NOT PANIC. Get up from the pilot's seat, walk calmly to the back of the plane, fix the plane, calmly walk to the front of the plane, have a seat in the pilot's seat, and continue to fly the plane."* A leader is not a leader if they are not able to handle crisis. You will not convince me otherwise. The following excerpt comes from an article in Forbes, entitled "How Training Like A Pilot Will Set You Up For Success In Crisis Management," by Robert Glazer, *"Pilots engage in some of the most rigorous training of any profession. They constantly prepare for disastrous situations and practice maneuvers that are unlikely to occur, such as landing a plane with one engine. While most of us will never face these situations, there is a core principle that pilots are taught for handling emergencies that we could all learn from: the ANC protocol. The ANC protocol stands for Aviate, Navigate and Communicate, in that order.*

- *Aviate — Maintain control of the aircraft*
- *Navigate — Know where you are and where you intend to go*
- *Communicate — Let someone know your plans and needs"*[13]

Communication comes after gaining control and figuring out what needs to be done. This takes place inside the mind and heart of a leader. Communication is not needed any time before that. It will only cause panic. Just imagine, if you will, staying with the plane example, how much panic and chaos would erupt if a pilot jumped right to communicating issues to the passengers on board. The energy alone would bring down the plane. We underestimate energy so much. It is critical for the pilot to take control, navigate, and then release information as needed. I highly recommend you research crisis tactics and even examine the military, which deals with crisis situations all the time. The better equipped you are to handle crises, the more successful you will be in life and in business. Whatever you do, DO NOT PANIC!

There is great power in remaining calm. I want you to remember this, not just in business, but also in your daily life. You are the leader of your life. Make sure to stay calm when emotions run high. I need you to fully activate your emotional intelligence and use every drop of it. When crises arise, and they will time and time again, I need you to take control of them. I need you to look at them with a clear mind. Therefore, being sober-minded is very important. Calm is your superpower. Let's take a closer look at that. The following are definitions from the dictionary:

- **Calm** is having the absence of strong emotions.

- **Super** refers to an extraordinary ability.
- **Power** is the capacity and size of your influence.

So how do you truly stay calm under pressure? It starts with your overall character. It starts with your thought process. There is great power in positive thinking. Most great leaders who operate out of a calm demeanor have an incredible mind. They are very positive in thought and in nature. American philosopher and psychologist William James once said, *"The greatest weapon against stress is our ability to choose one thought over another."* When stressful thoughts come into your mind, you must release them. You must not give way to them because they are cancerous and will multiply like gremlins. You need to avoid them, just like you need to avoid negative people. They, too, can cause you great stress. Energy is real. It is important as a leader that you are careful with your energy—what you give off and what you receive—especially during a time of crisis.

"It takes 20 years to build a reputation and only five minutes to ruin it. If you think about that, you will do things differently."

—Warren Buffett, billionaire investor

Warren Buffett is the business! Just as I have been a leader since I came out of the womb, so too, has Warren Buffett been an incredible businessman since conception. Did you know that he reads something like five to six hours a day according to some reports? Do you know what he is reading? Do you know why he reads so much? He is reading newspapers and corporate reports. His net worth is 77.7 Billion DOLLARS. Hello somebody. Buffett's leadership style is transformational. He has over 300,000 employees that he inspires, and whose lives are transformed by being under his leadership.

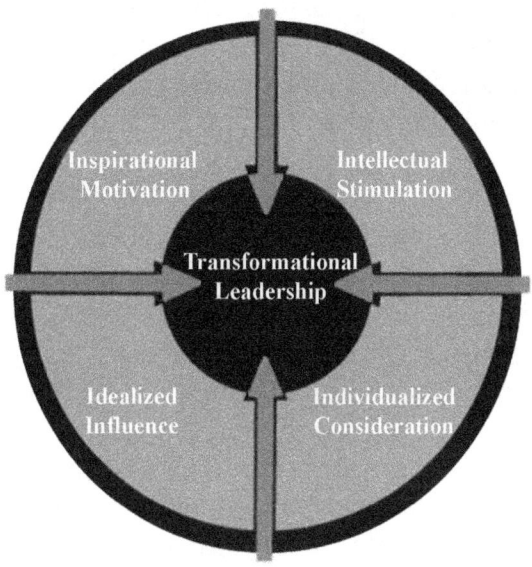

Created by Entrepreneurship Empowered based on Transformational Leadership Theory; Downton and Burns

What exactly is **transformational leadership**, you may ask? According to STU Online, *"Transformational leadership inspires people to achieve unexpected or remarkable results. It gives workers autonomy over specific jobs, as well as the authority to make decisions once they have been trained.*

Some of the basic characteristics of transformational leadership are inspirational, in that the leader can inspire workers to find better ways of achieving a goal; mobilization, because leadership can mobilize people into groups that can get work done, and morale, in that transformational leaders raise the well-being and motivation level of a group through excellent rapport. They are also good at conflict resolution."[14]

I share this leadership style with you because, as social entrepreneurs, you will need to inspire your people around the mission and vision of your social enterprise. Leadership is a mastery. An art, one could even say. Leadership, however, is dying. Why? Because we are leading by what we don't know more often than leading by what we do know. The wisdom of one cannot support the minds of many. It is only when each of us can use our gifts that we are able to be amazingly powerful. This is the challenge of a social enterprise leader. They must understand what dots connect the physical and the energetic realm. They must be able to bring to use the power of humanity as a driving force. This is most often done in a place of humility. This is done in a place of calmness. This is done in a place of deep thought and strategic placement of each person. I am a powerful leader, but I can promise you this much: it is my people who possess the greatest power of all. "*We the people...*" one of the most powerful statements in the U.S. But also one of the most underused resources. We must empty ourselves out and give way to our greatness. We must remove all forms of toxic thought and relationships in order to keep ourselves in tune with our highest frequency. It was that frequency that caused Ali to be the greatest boxer of all time. It's that frequency that will allow you to be the greatest version of yourself. It is that same power that will make an IMPACT in this world and the world still yet to come.

"In business, the most important lesson I have learned is that there is one currency that always plays the key role in forming value, and that is human capital—the knowledge, skills and experiences of people."

—Lowell Milken, international businessman and philanthropist

I started the chapter by stating you were in the human economy. I need you to understand you are to benefit, uplift, encourage, and empower that economy, starting with yourself. The way out is within. The more you develop yourself, the better you will be able to serve others. Without your human capital, you really don't have a business. I could not have grown my business the way I did without my human capital. The work you are doing as a social entrepreneur will require you to have solid human capital. According to Investopedia, *"human capital is an intangible asset or quality not listed on a company's balance sheet. It can be classified as the economic value of a worker's experience and skills. This includes assets like education, training, intelligence, skills, health, and other things employers' value such as loyalty and punctuality. The concept of human capital recognizes that not all labor is equal. But employers can improve the quality of that capital by investing in employees—the education, experience, and abilities of employees all have economic value for employers and for the economy as a whole. Human capital is important because it is perceived to increase productivity and thus profitability. So, the more a company invests in its employees (i.e., in their education and training), the more productive and profitable it could be."*

Your human capital is managed by your human resources (HR) department, which, for my business, was me. Although, I did have an accountant who took care of my employee taxes and payroll. I didn't have anyone else who helped, and certainly no department. I, however, was not that large of a business. At my peak, I had about seventeen staff members. I was able to handle all that was required with regard to HR. Each business will differ with regard to the needs of HR, but there will be a very common theme with all businesses: there will always be a recruiting and selection process. You will need to create job descriptions prior to posting job announcements. The job description should be detailed. It is important to be sure to include certain elements in your job posting that are mission-critical to the job—like lifting, typing, software comprehension, and so on. You also need to indicate you are a social enterprise and you are mission-driven. You will want to attract those whose values are in alignment with yours.

You will get a string of résumés submitted. Many times, employers will get hundreds of résumés a day. Depending on the economy, that is. But overall, people are always looking for work. Finding good help is very hard, however. You will go through all the résumés submitted and narrow them down by those who fit the job description. After you have selected your three to five potential candidates, you will then move into the interview process. It is good practice to have a set of standard interview questions. This makes the interviewing process fair for all candidates. Your questions should include questions pertaining to the job in which the candidate is being interviewed. You will also want to have questions that deal with conflict resolution. Behavior questions are critical, too, because they will tell you if the person will fit in with your work culture. Not everyone is fitted for your culture, and that is important to understand. As a social enterprise, you will want some ethical dilemma-based questions. They are just as important as all the other questions. You want an ethical person working for you. You are a social enterprise, and it will not work if you have an unethical staff.

After the interview, you will then move into making the selection, checking references, moving forward with an offer, and finally hire. This is where the paperwork madness comes into play. New hire paperwork will consist of government-required forms such as the I-9 and W-4. You can go directly to IRS.gov and pull the forms you need. They have a forms section, and the IRS website is fairly user-friendly. The forms are where a person will indicate the number of deductions they will be claiming, which indicates the amount of taxes that will be taken from one's income. Also, you will need to ensure you have an Employer Identification Number (EIN). You must have that in order to have employees but not to hire contractors, which is also an option. Contractors are not employees, and they require a scope of work, but you may want to consider taking on contractors versus employees. You will need to do further research on contractors, and if you take one of my classes at the college, I will go into more detail regarding them and the gig economy. You will need an EIN to have employees, and in the back of the book, I have provided further information on how to apply for an EIN.

Another important piece of the new hire process is clearly laying out how compensation works and how and when they will be paid. Most payments are now done by direct deposit. You may want to consider this as a way of paying your staff. In order to make direct deposits, you will not only need to have employees fill out a form, but you will need their banking information as well. The form they fill out will allow you to have access to their account for the sole purpose of depositing funds. A lot of employers will also give employees a schedule showing exactly when payday occurs. This helps employees manage their money and the bills they have to pay.

You will also need to think about benefits. There are required benefits, no matter the size of your business. According to the SBA, those benefits are:

- "***Social Security taxes***: *Employers must pay Social Security taxes at the same rate as their employees*
- **Workers' Compensation**: *Required through a commercial carrier, self-insured basis, or state Workers' Compensation Program*
- **Disability Insurance**: *Disability pay is required in California, Hawaii, New Jersey, New York, Rhode Island, and Puerto Rico*
- **Leave benefits**: *Most leave benefits are optional outside those stipulated in the Family and Medical Leave Act (FMLA)*
- **Unemployment insurance:** *Varies by state, and you may need to register with your state workforce agency*"[4]

Health insurance is another benefit that employers offer. I only had part-time employees, so I didn't offer health insurance. However, if you do have full-time employees, you will need to consider offering them health insurance. I highly recommend you do research not only on the Affordable Care Act, but on all the different types of health care plans available for employers. Below you will find additional bullet points of all that I have covered so far, plus a little more. The following information comes directly from Workable, a recruiting software company. They help you find, track, and hire employees.

- "*An employment contract should include:*

- - *Job information (job title, department)*
  - *Work schedule*
  - *Length of employment*
  - *Compensation and benefits*
  - *Employee responsibilities*
  - *Termination conditions*
- *Most common types of employment forms to complete are:*
  - *W-4 form (or W-9 for contractors)*
  - *I-9 Employment Eligibility Verification form*
  - *State Tax Withholding form*
  - *Direct Deposit form*
  - *E-Verify system: This is not a form, but a way to verify employee eligibility in the U.S.*
- *Possible internal forms.*
  - *Non-compete agreements*
  - *Non-disclosure agreements*
  - *Employee invention forms*
  - *Employee handbook acknowledgement forms*
  - *Drug and/or alcohol test consent agreements*
  - *Job analysis forms (responsibilities, goals and performance evaluation criteria)*
  - *Employee equipment inventory lists*
  - *Confidentiality and security agreements*
- *Most common employee benefits are:*
  - *Life and health insurance*
  - *Mobile plan*
  - *Company car*
  - *Stock options*
  - *Retirement plan*
  - *Disability insurance*
  - *Paid time off/vacation policies (including any paid holidays)*
  - *Sick leave*
  - *Employee wellness perks (e.g., gym memberships)*
  - *Tuition reimbursement*

- *Obtain employees' personal data for emergencies*
- *Emergency contacts*
- *Brief medical history*"[15]

    You will need to safeguard all the information you have on your staff. You will need to have locked cabinets or even an encrypted virtual file storage. It is your job to keep your records safe. There are many parts to the hiring process. You should have some type of onboarding process where new employees come in to not only do paperwork but receive training. The onboarding process is a magical time for the new hire. They are now beginning to see how your organization is being managed. This will tell them a lot. If you are not well managed, they may think they have made the wrong decision to work for you. You will need to ensure all that you provide your new hire is up to date, relevant, and that you also fully engage them in your culture. This is the time to really showcase your mission and all your company stands for. Your new hire said yes because they believe their purpose aligns with your mission. They believe they are there to help make an IMPACT with you. Make sure you don't let them down by not having a system for your new hires.

    I would now like you to take some time to think about all that we have covered in regard to human capital, HR, and onboarding. Go do some research on other social enterprises and see how they operate when it comes to their people. Then, I would like you to make some notes about how you would like to manage this part of your business. I would also like you to think about what type of onboarding process you will have. Now is your time to draft some possibilities for what awaits you in the future.

_____

_____

_____

_____

"Volunteers don't get paid, not because they're worthless, but because they're priceless."

—Sherry Anderson, Canadian curler

The STEEL Legacy is highly dependent on volunteers, and if you take the nonprofit route, you will also be dependent on volunteers. I personally love to volunteer, and if I could do it all the time and still make ends meet, I would. Truth is, volunteers do not get paid. However, that doesn't mean they don't hold tremendous value, because they do. According to the article "Volunteers: What Can They Do For You Today?" by David G. Phillips, *"Volunteers are of huge value to nonprofit organizations. Recent studies estimate that about a hundred million people volunteer each year with an annual value in the range of $150 billion. Not only do volunteers help to save money, but they can provide better service to clients, increase contact with the greater community, make available better expertise, and reduce costs of services."*[16] You will need to go through a similar process with regard to recruiting and staffing volunteers as you would with recruiting employees. Your volunteer screening may consist of the following:

- Volunteer applications
- Background checks
- References
- Interviews

You will need to remember that with volunteers, you need quality over quantity. Therefore, you will need to be sure your recruiting process is solid. This will ensure that you are finding the best volunteers possible. Many nonprofits do hire their volunteers for other paid staff jobs or special projects. Being able to truly count on your volunteers is priceless. It requires a lot of work each quarter I have an outreach. My volunteers will show up the night before to help me assemble the bags, and when we make sack lunches, they arrive early in the morning the day of the event. I can remember many times assembling them myself. Today, I have dedicated volunteers I can count on. I cannot tell you how much that means to me and the work I have been called to do. They believe in the mission of the STEEL Legacy. They are completely on board with supporting and assisting as needed. Volunteers are extremely special. They, too, will need to be taken care of. You don't pay them, but you could provide them with a volunteer *thank you* dinner or luncheon. You could give them small gifts of appreciation. You will need to ensure you are always kind to them and let them know you appreciate their service. Just like employees need to be motivated, so do volunteers. Make sure you do some research regarding how to manage and care for employees. Social enterprises will have volunteers. Keep in mind they are there because they truly believe in your cause. They truly believe in your mission, and they truly believe in your IMPACT.

Chapter 8
Leaving a Legacy

"The great use of life is to spend it for something that will outlast it."

—William James, American philosopher

Congratulations, you have made it to the final chapter. If you recall me stating in the Introduction that this chapter may bring you to tears, indeed, it just may. It brings me to tears just to write. As I type right now, tears are welling up in my eyes. The topic of legacy and passing on are not easy ones to speak about, let alone write about it. However, they are important topics. We will all turn to dust. Not one of us gets to stay. Nor do I believe we really would want to stay. That is simply not our fate as human beings. We die. We only die once. You see, we don't live once. No, we only die once. Make sure to live your life to the fullest. Go to the ultra-limits. Read books you have never read. Go to places you have never been to. Eat food you have never had.

Expand your mind and your life experiences. You are to make an IMPACT in this world, regardless if you are going to be a social entrepreneur or not. You still can and will leave your mark if you continue to live the EMPOWERED LIFE. What does it mean to be EMPOWERED? The dictionary defines empowered as *"made (someone) stronger and more confident, especially in controlling their life and claiming their rights."* You are to claim your rights to your life and to your dreams. You are to walk in confidence and love. You are to be your authentic self because you are amazing.

I love the quote I started this chapter with. As social entrepreneurs, not only are we in pursuit of making an IMPACT, but we are also pursuing a lasting legacy. We are trying to build something that will outlast us—a business that is timeless. One that will serve 100 generations, if not more. At least, that is my pursuit. My publishing company, Eternal Enterprise Publishing, and all the writing I have to date are all pieces of my lasting legacy. They are combined with my homeless and trauma work. I own 100% of my writings. My seeds can take my work and reproduce it and make it theirs and benefit from it. One thing I know is we will always have business. My first book, *Entrepreneurship Empowered*, is essentially a business guide similar to this book. My job before I depart will be to press a blueprint to show them what to look for in the future. This blueprint will require me to time travel just a bit. I will do my best to lay out a plan that will show them how to move the work through and add to the work as the generations continue to come. Boom! One hundred generations changed, if not more. At least, that is the plan.

In addition to my work that will be able to reproduce, they, too, can publish their own work if they choose to do so. My daughter is already a little book writer and an amazing artist. I can see that she will write books in the future and do great things with her art. My son is an incredible manager and growing in his leadership. I hold great faith in him to lead the company and ensure it is properly cared for.

I know they both will continue to build upon the legacy and, in turn, it will last. One of the things I share with my children is to remember that even though we will have great wealth, we are never to forget where we came from. We are here to serve humankind. To love and care for them. We are to stay humble and be a servant. I made them promise me they would be sure to teach their seeds this and ensure that they, too, agree to our family code.

In addition to the Eternal Enterprise Publishing, they will also have the STEEL Legacy. My goal before I depart is to have a foundation that supports the homeless with shelter, personal needs, clothing, food, employability skills, and the list goes on. My son has been serving with me since I started in 2003, and my daughter has been serving since conception. They both love to serve and have eyes that see the homeless. They have amazing hearts and truly care for others. I promise you this is by far the greatest thing I could leave them with, outside of one other critical aspect of life: the breaking of generational curses. I know that in my life, I have been chosen to break generational curses and plant generational blessings. I do not take that job lightly. It is not an easy job. But I am a Lion. I am CALLED.

You, too, have been called. I encourage you to take a moment and truly reflect on the generational curses in your own family. We all have a bloodline of trauma and a bloodline of curses—some more extreme than others. I refuse to pass abuse, poverty, and despair on to my children. No, it stops with me. I am EMPOWERED, and I will not allow another generation to come from me to suffer as I have. This topic is a deep one for me, and it has many layers to it. It is a great part of my work as a trauma expert—to expose the truth of how we pass on not only our problems, but our sicknesses and our traumas. For example, heart disease runs in a family. So, then, all the people in that family believe they will have heart disease. I need people to stand up and say, "Oh, hell no, it is not running through me. I am healthy and well. I am going to ensure I take care of my heart." I need people to fully understand that roughly

90% of our health issues are related to childhood and adult trauma.

According to an article titled, "Understanding How Trauma Affects Health and Health Care," by the Center for Health Care Strategies, *"experiencing trauma causes the body to produce adrenaline and cortisol, activating normal protective processes of fight, flight, or freeze. Unresolved traumatic experiences can stimulate these responses even in non-threatening situations. Experiencing trauma, especially in childhood, can actually change a person's brain structure, contributing to long-term physical and behavioral health problems. Children and adults often develop coping mechanisms to alleviate the pain of trauma, some of which are classified as 'health risk behaviors.' These can include eating unhealthy food or overeating, using tobacco, abusing substances, or engaging in risky sexual activities. When childhood traumatic stress goes untreated, these coping mechanisms can contribute to anxiety, social isolation, and chronic diseases like hypertension, diabetes, cancer, or substance use disorders."*[17]

The curse of trauma that is passed down from one generation to the next is one that I will spend my life fighting to expose and bring light to. It is my greatest social work. I have already seen great fruit from that work, as many people come to me and share with me how my life has helped save theirs—that my story has helped them to hold no shame. I would suffer all over again for all those who have already come, and those who are still yet to come. This is the blessing. I am actively planting blessings for my children and for future generations to come. I believe my greatest reward will be when those future generations come and see me in Heaven one day and say, "You, you were the one who broke the chain, you were the one who changed the entire direction of our legacy. You were the one who saved us..." And to that, I will say, "The way out is within." You see, I was just doing what I was called to do. This was always a part of the contract I signed. I am ever so grateful I never gave up the ghost in the despair of my depression and pain. That I found the strength to get up and fight for my life. That to this day, I still continue to do the work needed to be healed and free. It requires a lot of work to pull the bloodline of trauma off of your body and your legacy. It takes a lot of work to see the wicked problems in the world and take them on. I encourage you to rest when you need to, but don't ever give up on your purpose and why you have been placed on this earth. It is to make an IMPACT!

"All good men and women must take responsibility to create legacies that will take the next generation to a level we could only imagine."

—Jim Rohn, entrepreneur, author, and speaker

Dan Rockwell, a leadership expert in Pennsylvania, lists ten ways to build a legacy in his article titled, "10 Ways to Build Powerful Legacy Now."

1. *"Dare to be joyful. Serve in ways that bring you joy. Angry, unhappy people leave sad legacies.*
2. *Monitor your impact on others. What are you doing when you make the biggest difference? Do more of that.*
3. *Develop and maximize your talent, strengths, and skills. Know yourself – Bring yourself.*
4. *Do what matters now. Everyone who's at the end of life says it goes by fast.*
5. *Seize small opportunities. Big may follow. Stop waiting to make a difference.*
6. *Start with those closest to you and the ones you spend the most time with.*
7. *Bring your best self to work and family. Everyone has at least two selves. Bring out the best one.*
8. *Think service not success.*
9. *Relax. Don't run around building a legacy. Run around making a difference.*
10. *Elevate the needs of others over your own."*[18]

I really love all ten. As social entrepreneurs, they are all fitting. As EMPOWERED individuals, they are just as fitting. You see, no matter which path you choose—whether you go into entrepreneurship or not—I need you to be living the EMPOWERED LIFE. When I started this chapter, I shared the definition of EMPOWERED. Well, now you are going to write your own empowered statement. I want you to take some time now to reflect on all that we have covered in this chapter—from the building of a lasting legacy to the breaking of curses and planting of blessings. Then, I want you to write your EMPOWERED statement. I am going to share mine with you, then provide space for you to write your own. I will close out the chapter with a few more words of encouragement and one of the most powerful activities yet. Let's begin the EMPOWERMENT process.

Empowered Statement—My Example:
I am a people-pleaser, and many times I have become so hurt by family, friends, and people in general. What I am learning is that it is very unhealthy to be a people-pleaser. It can actually make you sick. The side effects of abuse are nothing nice. Being a people-pleaser is one of my side effects. But I am healing and will continue to heal and be free. I have decided to be EMPOWERED and no longer subject myself to people-pleasing. I will choose to say "no" and have no remorse. I will say "YES" to me! I am confident in myself and the purpose of my life. I know that I am not able to please everyone, nor will I inspire everyone, but I have had visions where I have seen seas upon seas of people who will be inspired by my life story. I will be used to give hope to so many who feel hopeless. I will be used to help others heal and set them free. This pleases me.

Now, you give it a try....

_____

_____
_____
_____

Before I close out this chapter, I would like to take the time now to express my gratitude to you. I am extremely grateful to you for being with me on this journey. I am confident that no matter what direction you decide to take in life, you will make an IMPACT. I am honored that you would read my writing, and if you are one of my students, I want you to know how incredibly honored I am to be your professor. To walk with you and support you on your educational journey. I believe I have given you all a wealth of information in this book. I hope you will come back time and time again to use what has now been revealed to you. What I love about being an author is, in my writings, I have found eternal life. I am confident my work will be shared with the world, and, more importantly, it will guide my seeds into seeds forevermore. This, my friends, is how you not only break generational curses, but this is how you plant generational blessings.

It took me many years to finally pull the muzzle off my mouth and live out loud. I have an extraordinary God-given talent, which is to give others a very special gift: the gift of self. Yes, you read that right. I give you the tools to help you find your authentic self. In doing so, I have given you everything you need. Like a domino effect, after you truly grasp hold of the gift of you, everything else will fall into place. I firmly believe the call-to-action activities you have encountered thus far have revealed a deeper you. I hold great confidence in the one you just did, which activated your EMPOWERMENT, and the one I am now going to leave you with: the writing of a legacy letter.

Writing a legacy letter is one of the hardest things I have ever done. While earning my master's degree, a professor gave us the assignment to write a legacy letter. I had never heard of such a thing. I can clearly see myself weeping like a baby at my desk as I wrote my son a final goodbye. You see, that is what a legacy letter is. It is a letter from you to your legacy—to your family and friends. You project yourself to your death bed and you write. It can be very hard, emotionally, because no matter how strong your faith is, the sting of death is very real. We all will cross it one day. I am a true believer that love is the only thing that is real; everything else is an illusion. Love never dies, but it does transcend, as each of us will do one day. I believe we have been given one commission here on earth, and that is to love, and we screw it up every day and three times on Sunday. This is why I share my message. This is why I live out loud. This is why the EMPOWERED series is within me. It is in my writings that I get to live—and the same is true for you. So, I encourage you to write. I desire to see you live the EMPOWERED LIFE. This is why I give you key after key to help set you free. Though this call-to-action activity is hard and may be difficult to do, I encourage you to write the letter. Go to your death bed, what type of life did you live? What do you want to say to your children and loved ones? What do you wish to say to the future generations still yet to come? What stories, values, wisdom, and blessings do you wish to share? Just write what comes to you. Again, I thank you for being on this journey with me. I pray that you write the letter and receive yet another key. Remember, the way out is within. Go within and write the letter, then go and live the EMPOWERED LIFE.

EMPOWERED LIFE™

Why Statement and Vision Board

Visionaries are able to manifest. Vision boards are a great way to manifest your vision. I have several vision boards. I have seen many things come to fruition through my boards. When I create them, I not only think about the vision, but I have learned how to feel the vision bringing the heart and the mind together. If you are believing in rain for the desert, you must not just pray for it, you must feel the rain. You must smell the rain. You must be wearing rain gear and be prepared for the rain. This is really the heart of vision. The feeling of it. If you truly want to succeed at making an *IMPACT,* then you need to not only see yourself and your business succeeding, you need to feel it. You need to feel what it is like to wear imported silk suits. You need to feel what it is like to sit at the top of your high-rise office building. The feeling is the part that brings it to life.

There are several ways you can create your vision board. You can gather magazines and cut out pictures or words. You will need glue sticks and a poster board to place the pictures on. You can also use a computer and google different things that represent your vision and then save the pictures. You then take those pictures and place them in a Word document. You could even create it in Adobe Photoshop. You could use your smartphone (same concept as with a computer). Google the things you desire for yourself, business, life, family, and so on. Then save the pictures to your camera roll. You then will need a collage maker—there are many free apps out there that can make picture collages. Then, place whichever pictures you like in the collage. TA-DA! You now have your vision board.

While creating the vision board, you really want to be connected in thought and heart. See yourself in the boat that you just cut out. Feel the breeze as you walk the beach and watch the sunset in the picture of Bali that is now on your board. See the increase in financial freedom, and see that you are rich in love, time, talents, and the like. I use a lot of words in my vision boards, as words are my love language.

What is your love language? If it is words, then make sure to use lots of positive words on your board.

The vision board needs to be placed where you can see it every day. If you created one with your phone, you could save it as your lock screen or background screen. You could even send it to be printed as a photograph. For your Word document boards, you can print them out in color, but black and white will do. The poster board method is simple: just put that sucker up on your wall. Put them all up on your wall. Look at them. Let them breathe and live within you. Go back to feeling your vision and believing in it. Before you know it, you will be driving the Camaro you put on your board. You will be floating in a hot air balloon ride. You will be walking the streets of Rome. All of what I just listed, from the Camaro to Rome, were on my vision board and have come to reality. I could go on and on, but now I want you to give it a try.

Please remember this one thing: the vision is for an appointed time. Though it may tarry, it will not be late. For everything there is a season. You must be patient and just know that your vision will come to pass if you faint not.

Steps to Form an LLC

According to Nolo, here are the steps you need to take to form an LLC.

1. *"Choose an LLC name.* The name of your business cannot be the same as the name of another limited liability company (LLC) on file with your state's LLC office (which is usually part of the same division as corporations, often the Secretary of State's office). The name must end with an LLC designator, such as "Limited Liability Company" or "Limited Company," or an abbreviation of one of these phrases ("LLC," "L.L.C.," or "Ltd. Liability Co.").

2. *File articles of organization.* Prepare and file "articles of organization" with your state's LLC filing office. Typically, you must provide only your LLC's name, its address, and sometimes the names of all of the owners—called members.

3. *Create an LLC operating agreement.* The LLC operating agreement contains rules for the ownership and operation of the business (much like a partnership agreement or corporate bylaws). A typical operating agreement includes the members' percentage interests in the business, the members' rights and responsibilities, and information on voting, management, and profits and losses.

4. *Publish a notice (AZ and NY only).* This step does not apply to LLC's in most states. If you are forming an LLC in Arizona or New York, you must take an additional step to make your company official: You must publish in a local newspaper a notice stating that you intend to form an LLC. Your local newspaper should be able to help you with this filing.

5. *Obtain licenses and permits.* Before you begin doing business, you need to obtain the required licenses and permits that anyone needs to start a new business. Among the licenses and permits you may need to obtain are a business license and, if your LLC will sell products, a seller's permit.

6. *Retain your limited liability.* To retain your LLC's status as a separate entity, LLC owners (members) must observe certain formalities, such as keeping detailed

financial records and recording minutes of major decisions."[19]

Remember to do your research to ensure you are making the best decision. Talk with accountants, financial advisors, and attorneys. Make sure you list all the pros and cons. Make sure you take a 360 degree look at your life, your product, your assets—both in business and in your personal life. Make sure you fully understand what the requirements are in your state for forming as an LLC.

Business Legal Structures

Because the business structures are perplexing, I have defined them again for you below. These definitions come directly from the SBA.

"A **sole proprietorship** is a business that is owned and usually operated by one person. It is the oldest, simplest, and cheapest form of business ownership because there is no legal distinction made between the owner and the business.

A **partnership** is two or more people voluntarily operating a business as co-owners for profit. Partnerships make up more than 8 percent of all businesses in the United States and more than 11 percent of the total revenue.

A **C corporation** is an artificial person created by law, with most of the legal rights of a real person. These include the rights to start and operate a business, to buy or sell property, to borrow money, to sue or be sued, and to enter into binding contracts. Corporations make up 20 percent of all businesses in the United States, but they account for almost 90 percent of the revenue.

S corporations are corporations that elect to pass corporate income, losses, deductions, and credits through to their shareholders for federal tax purposes. Shareholders of S corporations report the flow-through of income and losses on their personal tax returns and are assessed tax at their individual income tax rates. This allows S corporations to avoid double taxation on the corporate income. S corporations are responsible for tax on certain built-in gains and passive income at the entity level.

The limited liability company is a relatively new form of business ownership that is now permitted in all fifty states, although the laws of each state may differ. The LLC is a blend of a sole proprietorship and a corporation: the owners of the LLC have limited liability and are taxed only once for the business."[4]

Now for the legal business structures that must have some type of social endeavor: **Low-Profit Limited Liability Company**, also known as **L3C**. "A low-profit limited liability company (L3C) is a legal form of business entity in the

United States that was created to bridge the gap between non-profit and for-profit investing by providing a structure that facilitates investments in socially beneficial, for-profit ventures by simplifying compliance with Internal Revenue Service rules for program-related investments, a type of investment that private foundations are allowed to make."

The following information comes from the SBA. "***B corp.*** *A benefit corporation, sometimes called a B corp, is a for-profit corporation recognized in the majority of U.S. states. B corps are different from C corps in purpose, accountability, and transparency, but aren't different in how they're taxed. B corps are driven by both mission and profit.*

Nonprofit corporation. *Nonprofit corporations are organized to do charity, education, religious, literary, or scientific work. Because their work benefits the public, nonprofits can receive tax-exempt status, meaning they don't pay state or federal taxes income taxes on any profits they make."*[4]

Business Structure	Ownership	Liability	Taxes
Sole Proprietor	One Person	Unlimited Personal Liability	Personal Tax Only
Partnerships	Two or More People	Unlimited Personal Liability Unless Structured as a Limited Partnership	Self-Employment Tax (except for limited partnerships) Personal Tax
Limited Liability Company (LLC)	One or More People	Owners Are Not Personally Liable	Self-Employment Tax Personal Tax or Corporate Tax
Corporation C – Corp	One or More People	Owners Are Not Personally Liable	Corporate Tax
Corporation S – Corp	One or More People, But No More Than 100, and all must be U.S. Citizens	Owners Are Not Personally Liable	Personal Tax
Corporation B – Corp	One or More People	Owners Are Not Personally Liable	Corporate Tax
Corporation Nonprofit	One or More People	Owners Are Not Personally Liable	Tax-Exempt, But Corporate Profits Can't be Distributed

Created by Entrepreneurship Empowered based on information from SBA: Business Legal Structures

Business Plan Template

The following information comes directly from the SBA and is the more formal business plan template.

- *"Executive summary*
  - Briefly tell your reader what your company is and why it will be successful. Include your mission statement, your product or service, and basic information about your company's leadership team, employees, and location. You should also include financial information and high-level growth plans if you plan to ask for financing.
- *Company description*
  - Use your company description to provide detailed information about your company. Go into detail about the problems your business solves. Be specific, and list out the consumers, organization, or businesses your company plans to serve.
  - Explain the competitive advantages that will make your business a success. Are there experts on your team? Have you found the perfect location for your store? Your company description is the place to boast about your strengths.
- *Market analysis*
  - You'll need a good understanding of your industry outlook and target market. Competitive research will show you what other businesses are doing and what their strengths are. In your market research, look for trends and themes. What do successful competitors do? Why does it work? Can you do it better? Now's the time to answer these questions.
- *Organization and management*
  - Tell your reader how your company will be structured and who will run it.

- o *Describe the legal structure of your business. State whether you have or intend to incorporate your business as a C or an S corporation; form a general or limited partnership; or if you're a sole proprietor or LLC.*
- o *Use an organizational chart to lay out who's in charge of what in your company. Show how each person's unique experience will contribute to the success of your venture. Consider including résumés and CV's of key members of your team.*
- **Service or product line**
  - o *Describe what you sell or what service you offer. Explain how it benefits your customers and what the product lifecycle looks like. Share your plans for intellectual property, like copyright or patent filings. If you're doing research and development for your service or product, explain it in detail.*
- **Marketing and sales**
  - o *There's no single way to approach a marketing strategy. Your strategy should evolve and change to fit your unique needs.*
  - o *Your goal in this section is to describe how you'll attract and retain customers. You'll also describe how a sale will actually happen. You'll refer to this section later when you make financial projections, so make sure to thoroughly describe your complete marketing and sales strategies.*
- **Funding request**
  - o *If you're asking for funding, this is where you'll outline your funding requirements. Your goal is to clearly explain how much funding you'll need over the next five years and what you'll use it for.*

- o *Specify whether you want debt or equity, the terms you'd like applied, and the length of time your request will cover. Give a detailed description of how you'll use your funds. Specify if you need funds to buy equipment or materials, pay salaries, or cover specific bills until revenue increases. Always include a description of your future strategic financial plans, like paying off debt or selling your business.*
- **Financial projections**
    - o *Supplement your funding request with financial projections. Your goal is to convince the reader that your business is stable and will be a financial success.*
    - o *If your business is already established, include income statements, balance sheets, and cash flow statements for the last three to five years. If you have other collateral you could put against a loan, make sure to list it now.*
    - o *Provide a prospective financial outlook for the next five years. Include forecasted income statements, balance sheets, cash flow statements, and capital expenditure budgets. For the first year, be even more specific and use quarterly—or even monthly—projections. Make sure to clearly explain your projections and match them to your funding requests.*
    - o *This is a great place to use graphs and charts to tell the financial story of your business.*
- **Appendix**
    - o *Use your appendix to provide supporting documents or other materials were specially requested. Common items to include are credit histories, résumés, product pictures, letters of reference, licenses, permits, patents legal documents, permits, and other contracts."*[4]

Marketing Plan

The following information is from the SBA and is the most common marketing template.

- "*Target market*
  - Describe your audience in detail. Look at the market's size, demographics, unique traits, and trends that relate to demand for your business.
- *Competitive advantage*
  - Describe what gives your product or service an advantage over the competition. It might be a better product, a lower price, or an excellent customer experience. Sometimes, an environmentally friendly certification or "made in the USA" on your label can be an important factor for customers.
- *Sales plan*
  - Describe how you'll literally sell your service or product to your customers. List the sales methods you'll use, like retail, wholesale, or your own online store. Explain each step your customer takes once they decide to buy.
- *Marketing and sales goals*
  - Describe your marketing and sales goals for the next year. Common marketing and sales goals are to increase email subscribers, grow market share, or increase sales by a certain percent.
- *Marketing action plan*
  - Describe how you'll achieve your marketing and sales goals. List marketing channels you'll use, like online advertising, radio ads, or billboards. Explain your pricing strategy and how you'll use promotions. Talk about the customer support that happens after the sale. The federal government regulates advertising and labeling for a number of consumer products, so make sure your advertising is legally compliant.

- ***Budget***
    - *Include a complete breakdown of the costs of your marketing plan. Try to be as accurate as possible. You'll want to keep tracking your costs once you put your plan into action."*[4]

Income Statement, Balance Sheet, and Cash Flow

```
                  Entrepreneurship Empowered
                     Income Statement Model
                 January 1 through December 31, 20___
```

Net Sales...	$725,425	
Less: Cost of Goods Sold............................	456,740	
Gross Income...................................		$268,685
Operating Expenses:		
Salaries..	$125,698	
Utilities...	8,689	
Depreciation......................................	15,025	
Rent...	3,500	
Building Services.................................	5,985	
Insurance...	6,200	
Interest...	2,585	
Office Supplies...................................	13,259	
Sales Promotion..................................	16,120	
Taxes and Licenses...............................	6,848	
Maintenance......................................	1,258	
Delivery..	3,895	
Miscellaneous....................................	1,125	
Total Expenses................................		$210,187
Net Income Before Taxes...........................		58,498
Less: Income Taxes.................................		14,624
Net Income After Taxes............................		43,874

```
                  Entrepreneurship Empowered
                     Balance Sheet Model
                       December 31, 20___
```

Assets

Current Assets:			
Cash...	$ 8,758		
Accounts Receivable.............................	61,984		
Inventory...	82,054		
Prepaid Expenses................................	1,650		
Total Current Assets........................		$154,446	
Fixed Assets:			
Equipment..	$100,750		
Building..	54,965		
Gross Fixed Assets...........................		$155,715	
Less Accumulated Depreciation.............		19,985	
Net Fixed Assets.............................			136,730
Total Assets.......................................			$293,176

Liabilities and Owners' Equity

Current Liabilities:			
Accounts Payable................................	$62,482		
Accrued Payable.................................	1,640		
Total Current Liabilities....................		$67,122	
Long-Term Liabilities:			
Mortgage Payable................................		32,680	
Total Liabilities.............................			$ 99,802
Owners' Equity:			
Capital Stock.....................................		165,000	
Retained Earnings................................		28,374	
Total Equity.................................			193,374
Total Liabilities and Owners Equity.............			$293,176

```
                  Entrepreneurship Empowered
                   Cash Flow Statement Model
               For the Year Ended December 31, 20___
```

Cash Flow From Operations

Net Income..	89,500
Adjustments for depreciation............................	2,500
Adjustments for increased inventories..................	(25,000)
Adjustments for decrease in accounts receivable.......	13,000
Net Cash Flow from Operations..........................	68,300

Cash Flow from Investing

Cash receipts from sale of property and equipment....	12,000
Cash paid for purchase of equipment...................	(14,000)
Net Cash Flow from Investing...........................	(2,000)

Cash Flow from Financing

Cash paid for loan repayment............................	(6,500)
Net Cash Flow from Financing...........................	(6,500)

Net Increase in Cash	59,800

Accounting Terms & Definitions

Terms and definitions as defined by the dictionary:

Revenue: the value received by a firm in return for a good or service.

Expenses: the costs of labor, goods, and services.

Cost of goods sold: the total cost in terms of raw materials, labor, and overhead of the business that can be allocated to production.

Net income: the total revenue in an accounting period minus all expenses during the same period. If income taxes and interest are not deducted, it is called operating profit (or loss, as the case may be).

Assets: the things a business owns, includes cash, accounts receivable, inventory, equipment, building.

Current assets: cash and other assets that are expected to be converted to cash within a year.

Fixed assets: is a long-term tangible piece of property that a firm owns and uses in its operations to generate income. Fixed assets take longer than a year to convert to cash.

Accounts receivable: current assets resulting from selling a product on credit.

Goodwill (not the store): is a long-term (or noncurrent) asset categorized as an intangible asset.

Intangible assets: is an asset that is not physical in nature. Goodwill, brand recognition and intellectual property, such as patents, trademarks and copyrights, are all intangible assets.

Long-term investments: is an account on the asset side of a company's balance sheet that represents the company's investments, including stocks, bonds, real estate and cash that it intends to hold for more than a year.

Liabilities: is defined as a company's legal financial debts or obligations that arise during the course of business operations.

Current liabilities: are debts payable within one year.

Accounts payable: money owed by a company to its creditors.

Accrued expenses: are payments that a company is obligated to pay in the future for which goods and services have already been delivered.

Short-term debt: is an account shown in the current liabilities portion of a company's balance sheet. This account is made up of any debt incurred by a company that is due within one year.

Long-term debt: consists of loans and financial obligations lasting over one year. Long-term debt for a company would include any financing or leasing obligations that are to come due after a 12-month period.

Shareholder equity: also referred to as the owner's residual claim after debts have been paid, is equal to a firm's total assets minus its total liabilities.

Retained earnings: are the profits that a company has earned to date, less any dividends or other distributions paid to investors.

Capital stock: is the number of common and preferred shares that a company is authorized to issue, according to its corporate charter.

Employee Identification Number

If you plan to have employees, you are required by law to have an EIN. It is a very simple process. The following steps are how you file for and obtain an EIN. The following information comes directly from the IRS website (see below). As I have stated before, I highly suggest you explore both the SBA and IRS websites, as they will be two of your top resources in business.

1. *"Determine Eligibility: You may apply for an EIN online if your principal business is located in the United States or U.S. Territories. The person applying online must have a valid Taxpayer Identification Number (SSN, ITIN, EIN). You are limited to one EIN per responsible party per day. The 'responsible party' is the person who ultimately owns or controls the entity or who exercises ultimate effective control over the entity. Unless the applicant is a government entity, the responsible party must be an individual (i.e., a natural person), not an entity."*

2. Understand the Online Application: *"You must complete this application in one session, as you will not be able to save and return at a later time. Your session will expire after 15 minutes of inactivity, and you will need to start over."*

3. Submit Your Application: *"After all validations are done you will get your EIN immediately upon completion. You can then download, save, and print your EIN confirmation notice."*[20]

You see how simple that is? Now go to www.irs.gov and search for EIN, then read all that you find.

Answer Key

Kid Tested. Mother Approved.
Life's Good
Trusted Everywhere
Maybe She's Born With It
We Try Harder
Keep Walking
Gather 'Round the Good Stuff
Makes Mouths Happy
Something Special in the Air
It's Not Just a Job, It's an Adventure!

Kix Cereal — The famous low sugar, round cereal!
LG Electronics — LG manufactures high quality flat panel televisions.
Duracell Batteries — Called "The Coppertop"
Maybelline — Maybelline was started in 1915!
Avis — Avis is headquartered in Parsippany, New Jersey.
Johnnie Walker — Johnnie Walker Scotch Whiskey is produced in Scotland.
Pizza Hut — Pizza Hut is owned by the same company that owns Taco Bell.
Twizzlers — Twizzlers flavors include chocolate, strawberry, and watermelon.
American Airlines — American Airlines is headquartered in Ft. Worth, Texas.
Navy — The Department of the Navy is a division of the Department of Defense.

References and Resources

Excerpts and charts from *Entrepreneurship Empowered* were used in the writing of *IMPACT*.

The following resources were used in writing this book and are duly noted in the text:

[1] Swanbrow, Diane. "Empathy: College Students Don't Have as Much as They Used To." (2010.) University of Michigan News. Accessed January 12, 2020.
https://news.umich.edu/empathy-college-students-don-t-have-as-much-as-they-used-to/.

[2] Kidder, Rushworth M. 2009. *How Good People Make Tough Choices: Resolving the Dilemmas of Ethical Living*. Published by HarperCollins. New York, New York.

[3] Karan, Abraar. 2017. "A Doctor's Dilemma: A Case of Two 'Right' Answers." The Hastings Center. Accessed January 30, 2020.
https://www.thehastingscenter.org/doctors-dilemma-case-two-right-answers/

[4] Small Business Administration website:
www.sba.gov

[5] Berger, Jonah. (2016.) *Contagious: Why Things Catch On*. Published by Simon & Schuster. New York: New York.

[6] Przybyla, Dena. (n.d.) "The Psychology of Colors in Marketing and Branding." Accessed January 30, 2020.
https://www.colorpsychology.org/color-psychology-marketing/

[7] Active Marketing website:
https://www.activemarketing.com/our-work/.

[8] Conrardy, Alyssa. (2017.) "Build Your Social Enterprise Marketing Plan with This Template." Prosper Strategies. Accessed January 30, 2020.
https://prosper-strategies.com/social-enterprise-marketing-plan-template/.

[9] Kumar, Vineet. (2014.) "Making 'Freemium' Work." *Harvard Business Review*. Accessed January 30, 2020.
https://hbr.org/2014/05/making-freemium-work.

[10] Gauss, Allison. (n.d.) "There's More Than One Way to Fund a Nonprofit." Classy. Accessed January 30, 2020.
https://www.classy.org/blog/theres-more-than-one-way-to-fund-a-nonprofit/.

[11] Bidding Owl website:
https://www.biddingowl.com/.

[12] Ou, Amy Y., Waldman, David A., and Peterson, Suzanne J. "Do Humble CEOs Matter?" (2015.) *Journal of Management*. Accessed January 13, 2020.
https://createvalue.org/wp-content/uploads/Do-Humble-CEOs-Matter.pdf.

[13] Glazer, Robert. "How Training Like a Pilot Will Set You Up for Success." (2018.) Forbes. Accessed January 13, 2020.
https://www.forbes.com/sites/robertglazer/2018/07/13/how-training-like-a-pilot-will-set-you-up-for-success-in-crisis-management/#62059d1f7dde.

14 "What is Transformational Leadership? How New Ideas Produce Impressive Results." (2014.) STU online. Accessed January 13, 2020.
  https://online.stu.edu/articles/education/what-is-transformational-leadership.aspx.

15 Workable website:
  https://www.workable.com/.

16 Phillips, David G. (2018.) "Volunteers: What Can They Do For You Today?" CDS. Accessed January 30, 2020.
  https://blog.cdsfunds.com/volunteers_what_can_they_do_for_you.

17 Kuruna, Teagan. (2016.) "Understanding How Trauma Affects Health and Health Care." Center for Health Care Strategies. Accessed January 30, 2020.
  https://www.chcs.org/understanding-trauma-affects-health-health-care/.

18 Rockwell, Dan. (2014.) "10 Ways to Build Powerful Legacy Now." Leadership Freak. Accessed January 30, 2020.
  https://leadershipfreak.blog/2014/03/04/10-ways-to-build-powerful-legacy-now/.

19 Nolo website:
  https://www.nolo.com/.

20 Internal Revenue Service (IRS) website:
  https://www.irs.gov./.

About the Author

Ms. Palumbo is a business professional with more than 20 years of experience, 17 as an entrepreneur. She is a creative leader with in-depth knowledge and expertise applying strategic business management, development of small business initiatives, and progressive leadership. Ms. Palumbo is an effective communicator with an innate ability to engage and hold the attention of those she trains and teaches. She owns several businesses, and she successfully grew her core business into multiple states. She is a social entrepreneur and has been serving the homeless community for more than 16 years. In addition to being an Empowered Entrepreneur, Ms. Palumbo is a Business Adjunct professor for several colleges in the greater Sacramento region.

Natasha M Palumbo, MBA
Author, Coach, Consultant and Speaker
Entrepreneur – Educator – Empowered

Instagram and LinkedIn: Natasha M Palumbo

natasha@entrepreneurshipempowered.com

www.ingramcontent.com/pod-product-compliance
Lightning Source LLC
Chambersburg PA
CBHW032257150426
43195CB00008BA/483